New Patter
Honiton Lace

Flower Bower

New Patterns in Honiton Lace

Caroline and Barry Biggins

B.T. Batsford Ltd London

First published 1993
Reprinted 1994, 2001

Typeset by Goodfellow & Egan, Cambridge
and printed and bound in Spain by
Bookprint, S.L, Barcelona

Published by
B.T.Batsford Ltd
9 Blenheim Court
Brewery Road
London N7 9NT

A member of the Chrysalis Group plc.

A catalogue record for this book is available from the British Library

ISBN 0 7134 8647 3

Acknowledgements

We would like to thank all our friends and colleagues who have helped us to produce this book and whose names are given with each of the patterns they worked. Also our grateful thanks to Dr Anthony Copping, who patiently developed and printed the photographs

Contents

Flower Fountain

Introduction

The idea for a book of Honiton lace patterns came about when we won the 'John Bull' competition, run by the English Lace School, in 1986. The subject for the competition was 'Rings and Roundels' and I saw in my mind a bird alighting on a chain of hoops. The design was drawn by my husband and when he made another winning design entitled 'Celebrations' for a further 'John Bull' competition, it was clear that, although he knew nothing at all about lacemaking, he had definite ideas about lace design. All the designs in the book are his.

The patterns were given out to experienced lacemakers, who each interpreted the design in their own way. Many extremely interesting and inventive ideas have evolved and it became clear that there are as many different ways of working a pattern as there are lacemakers.

The most important aim of the book is to encourage experiment and invention. In this way Honiton lace will continue to develop and thrive.

It is not a book of technique and is intended for those with a knowledge of both flat and raised work. There is, however, a note after each pattern to help with general technical points.

The only fillings included are those not found in other lace books. The number of pairs used is not included for any piece, as this depends on the thread being used and individual preference.

Instructions are given on how the photographed lace is worked, with some alternative suggestions. The photographs are intended as a guideline only and where the designs do not exactly correspond because of the way the worker has interpreted the design, the drawing has been left in its original state, so that comparisons can be made.

We hope the book will stimulate ideas, especially for those who find it hard to draw their own designs.

Caroline Biggins

Raised and Rolled Work Exercise

Honiton lace is renowned for its raised work. The edge of any pattern can be raised, as the ribbed edge emphasizes the outline and enhances the work. The rib outline is worked first and the pattern filled in over the top, so that when the work is turned over, the edge is thrown into relief.

in. Work the pinhole at the tip and then turn the pillow to work back over the leaf.

All the sewings into the rib must be top or raised sewings, except where there is a pair that was laid to the back of the work. This pair attaches the work to the rib where it is brought in, instead of a sewing.

Pricking A. Correct Size Pricking

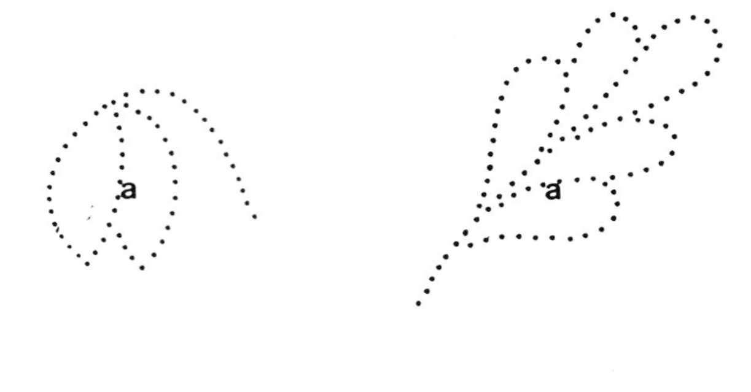

Diagram B. Bud and Leaf

Where there is an adjoining section of work, as in the bud and the leaf *a* (*see* Diagram B), where one row of holes serves both sections, the threads are rolled up the side of the completed braid and carried on into the next section.

The sampler is a first exercise in raised and rolled work and is described in detail.

Refer to Diagram C. Set up six pairs for the rib at [a], with pinholes on the right and the knots wound well back. Rib up as far as [b], which is the fourth pinhole from the tip of the bud. Hang in a pair here and lay it to the back of the work. Hang in a pair at the next two pinholes and lay them to the back of the work; also at the last pinhole before the tip, take the first downright pair past the pin and lay it to the back of the work, beside the last pair hung

After the top pinhole has been completed, work back through the first pair and tie the runners once, to keep the top pinhole from stretching. Work the runners through the rest of the downright pairs, bring in the pair that was laid to the back out of the rib and work through these, then bring in the pair that was hung in and laid back at this hole. Work the runners through this pair, leave the runners, tie the hung in pair once, twist this pair, change to half stitch and work back to the plain side. Add a pair here and on the next two holes on this side. Work back to the rib edge through all the downright pairs, now bring in the pair that was hung in and laid back at the third hole from the tip. Work the runners through this pair. Leave the runners and tie the hung in pair once, twist it and work back in

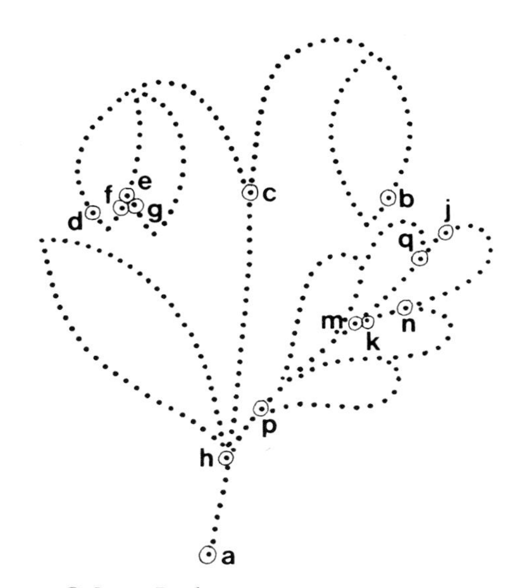

Diagram C. Large Pricking

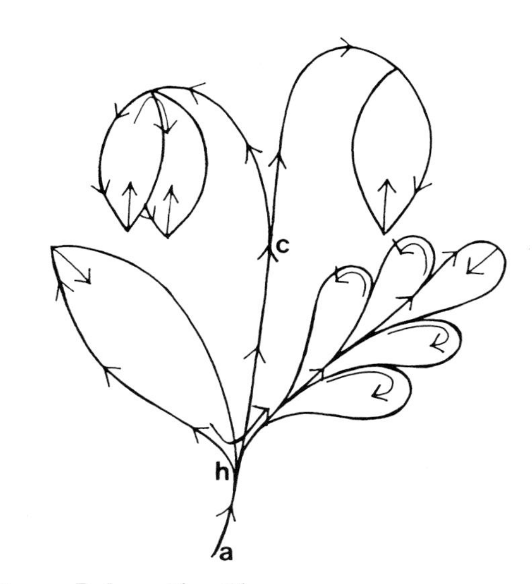

Diagram D. Large Flow Chart

half stitch to the plain side. When all the rib pinholes with hung in pairs have been used up, attach the runners to the rib with raised sewings.

Refer to Diagram E. The raised sewing is taken into the top or bottom bar of the pinhole, [a] or [b], *not* the outside edge as with an ordinary sewing.

If a back stitch has to be made at any time on the rib side – where the lines of weaving are not at right angles to the edge – a sewing can be taken into the top bar of the pinhole and then, in the next row, into the bottom bar of the same pinhole.

Work down to the bottom of the bud, reducing the pairs to six at the bottom. Save two thrown out pairs to make a tie back tassel with the bunch at the bottom.

Sew six rib pairs into the stem at [c] and rib round to [d], which is three holes from the tip of the bud. Hang in a pair to be laid back at the next two holes. At the last hole before the tip, lay back the first pair past the pin and complete this bud as for the first bud, reducing to six pairs at the bottom.

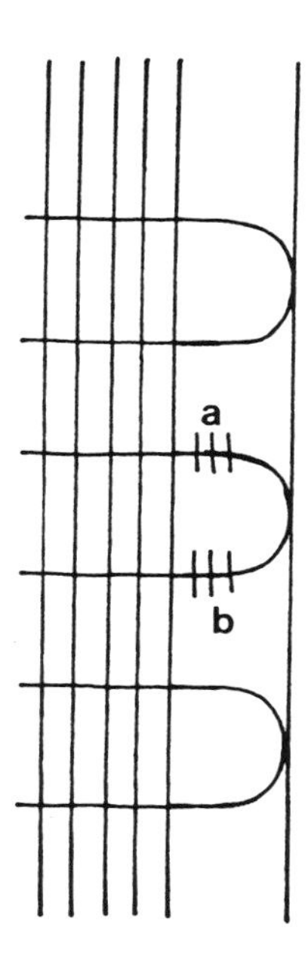

Diagram E. Raised Sewing

Raised and Rolled Work Exercise

Tie the pair that has done the final sewing at the bottom of the bud once. Leaving the pair of downrights on the right, i.e., the pair nearest the pinhole, lift the other four pairs and put them between the sewn pair, tie the sewn pair over the bunch twice and make a roll, holding this bunch in one hand and winding the sewn pair round the bunch to reach up as far as [e]. Sew the pair that has done the winding in at [f], tie it once, twist three times and leave it.

Now return to the pair left out of the bunch at the bottom and use it to stitch the roll to the completed bud. Put the needle pin into the bottom hole and make an ordinary sewing, catching one of the threads underneath the roll and putting the other bobbin over the top of the roll through this loop. Tie this pair once and use it to attach the roll all the way up to [e], sewing into each hole, under the roll and tying the pair once over the top of the roll.

On reaching [e], straighten out the bobbins of the bunch. Use the pair that has done the winding to weave through the straightened downrights to the pinhole side and put in the pin at [g]. Make up the edge stitch here, with the runner pair and the pair left at [f]. Three pinholes from the tip, start hanging in pairs and laying them to the back, as for the first bud. Turn at the tip and complete as for the first bud.

Sew in six rib pairs at [h] for the half stitch vein leaf and rib up the underside. At the seventh pinhole from the tip, hang in a pair and lay it to the back of the rib, hang in and lay back a pair at each of the next five pinholes. At the last pinhole before the tip, as well as hanging in a new pair, take the first downright pair past the pin and lay it to the back beside the last pair hung in, and complete the top pinhole.

Turn the pillow to work back over with ordinary pinholes on the plain side and raised sewings over the top of the rib, except where there is a pair hung in and laid to the back.

After making the first stitch, tie the runners once, to keep the top pinhole small and neat. Work through all the downright pairs, bring in the pair laid to the back of the work and work through these. Bring in the pair hung in at this hole and work the runners through this pair. Leave the runners and tie the hung in pair once. Use this pair to work as runners over to the plain side. Add another pair at each of the next six holes on this side and bring in the pairs hung in on each row, on the rib side.

Reduce to six pairs at the bottom of the vein leaf and work these pairs in rib across the stem and into the top of the tap leaf. Work up the stem with the pinholes on the right. At the fourth pin from the tip [j], hang in a pair and lay it to the back of the work. Do the same at the next two holes. At the last hole before the tip, the first downright pair past the pin is laid back beside the other hung in pairs. Turn at the tip and work down over the first tap leaf in whole stitch, adding two extra pairs on the plain side.

At the bottom of the tap, reduce to seven pairs. The last pinhole on the plain side [k] should be slightly higher than the last sewing into the rib [m].

After the last sewing into the rib, tie the sewn pair once and, leaving out the pair nearest to the rib side, lift the remaining five pairs and put them between the two bobbins of the sewn pair. Tie the sewn pair over the top of the bunch. Leave another pair on the left out of the bunch (this is useful in the next tap for filling in). Use the sewn and tied pair to wind round the bunch until it reaches [n]. Sew the winding pair into the pinhole above [n], tie it, twist three times and leave. Stitch the roll to the tap with the pair not tied into the bunch. Straighten the roll and rib to the top of the next tap using the pair that has done the sewing as runners to work through the straightened roll pairs. Make the end stitch with the pair sewn in above [n].

The taps are all worked in this way, bringing in the pair that was left out of the roll at [m] to fill in a little hole that may appear at this point.

On reaching [p] at the bottom of the last tap, reduce to six pairs. Top sew both runner pairs and tie them both once. Open one of the sewn pairs and put the other four between the sewn pair. Tie this pair and use it to roll round the bunch all the way up the side of the rib to [q]. The pair left behind is used to stitch the roll to the rib. Work the two remaining taps the same as the first side, finishing off with a tie back tassel.

THE PATTERNS

Rings and Roundels

1 Apple Tree

INTERPRETED BY PAULINE COCHRANE

Worked in 180 Thread

Working Notes

The many leaves of the tree are worked in two different ways. The whole and half stitch leaves are begun at the tip and worked straight down. More pairs are needed on the whole stitch side.

Where two leaves are directly opposite one another on either side of the stem, work the whole and half stitch leaf straight down, reduce pairs, cross over the braid and rib up the central vein of the opposite leaf. Tie, bunch and cut off the ends, leaving them long. Set up again at the tip of the whole stitch leaf. When work reaches the top of the vein, the runners are sewn into the rib. Work right over the vein, sewing in runners as they cross the rib.

The rib and braid branches are worked with two sets of bobbins so that they can merge in neatly (*see* Note 1).

Diagram 1

Working Order

1 Flowers. Rib central ring and carry pairs into the petals. Roll and rib each petal, hanging pairs in round the top of each petal for the half stitch backing.

2 Sew pairs into the flower at [a] and work pot rim, adding a coarse pair for the braid.

3 Rib round the outline of the pot.

4 Set up rib at [b]. Rib round the central scallop of the pot, hanging in pairs round the curve for filling in. Fill in scallop, sew out the middle pairs into the pot rim and use the outer edge pairs to roll up either side of the central scallop. Work the remaining scallops out to the edge both ways, outlining each in rib.

Apple Tree

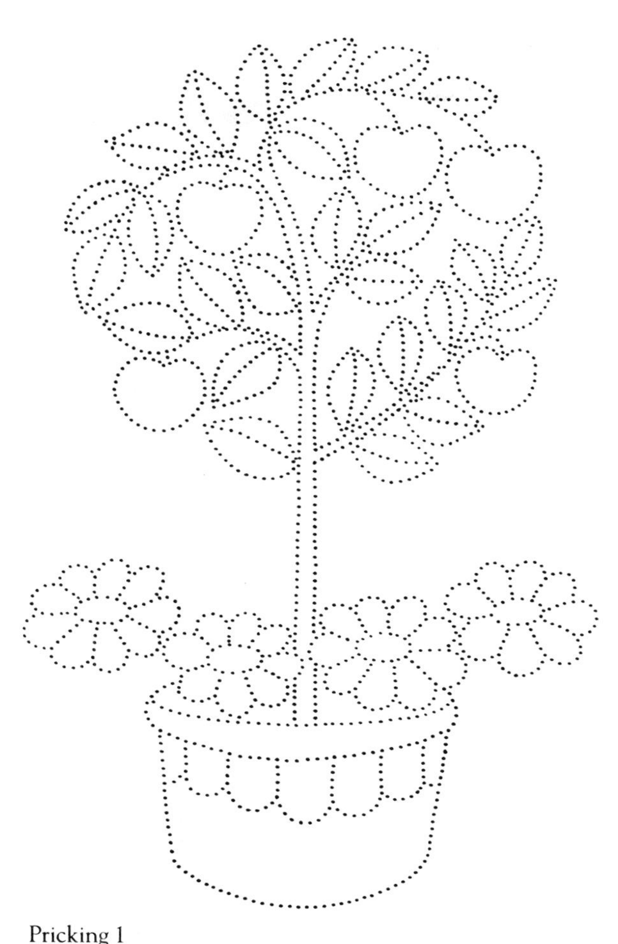

Pricking 1

5 Tree. Set up the rib at [c], rib round the apple and into the stem, leave the pairs hanging before they reach the rib from the apple [d]. Set up again at the apple [d], rib round and incorporate into the first stem. Work the leaf [e], join with the stem from [c]. Do likewise from the leaf [f], the apple [g] and the leaf [h]. Work the remaining leaves and apples.

Fillings

A No Pin.
B Toad in the Hole with Wide Headworks.

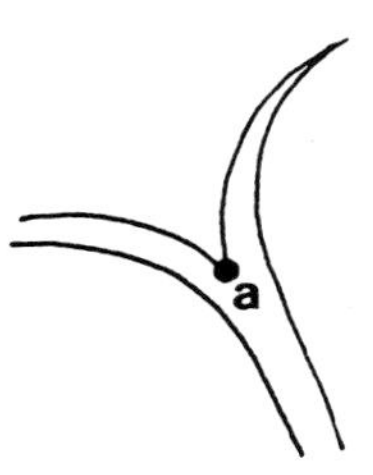

Diagram 1a

Note 1

Merging two braids. Refer to Diagram 1a. Work both braids down as far as [a]. Arrange work so that the outer holes are not made up in advance of [a]. Use the pairs from one side to make up the pinhole at [a]. Take the twists off the adjacent pairs, which are now touching at [a]. Make a whole stitch with them and leave these two pairs hanging. Work right across the row from the side with the two pairs of runners, i.e. the pairs not used to make up pinhole [a], through all the pairs, including the coarse pair. Work one more row before cutting out the coarse pair.

2 Bows and Bells

INTERPRETED BY PAULINE COCHRANE

Worked in 180 Thread

Bows and Bells

Working Notes

This is an example of how a pattern can be broken up and used as separate designs. The crown and central medallion between the ribbons could be omitted.

Getting the ribbon braids to flow is the main problem, and they can be worked in a variety of different ways.

Working Order

Bow

1 Begin half stitch knot at [1], work section [a], roll back to [1], work section [b]. Roll back to [1], work section [c].

2 Rib threads from section [c] along the bottom of ribbon [2]. Add a coarse pair where the rib becomes a braid, sew out into the knot. Work the inner ribbons.

3 Sew pairs into the knot for section [3], carry on into rib, cutting out the coarse pair, and sew into the completed ribbon [2]. Repeat for the other side.

4 Set up pairs at [d] with a coarse pair, cut the pair out for the small section of rib and hang it again for section [5].

Bows and Bells, upper section

Diagram 2

Pricking 2a

5 Work up to [e], roll threads down to [f]. Carry these pairs on into [6].

6 Add a coarse pair, work up to rib [g] and leave pairs hanging until [7] has been worked.

7 Sew pairs for [7] into ribbon [5], work up to [h], roll threads down to [j]. Sew out pairs left from rib [g].

8 Work the threads from [j] up to the knot, reduce to a rib and sew into knot.

9 Sew in pairs at [k] for ribbon [9], sew pairs into the knot, turn and use these pairs for ribbon [10].

10 Rib from knot to tip, turn and work back over. Repeat for the other side.

Crown

11 Begin rib for central ball at [m], work down, round ball and up into the top ball. Sew out into start.

12 Sew in pairs for scallops at [n], work across the top, outline each scallop, turn and fill in. Rib bottom of crown.

13 Set up at [p], work to centre, sew into central ball, roll back along work, rib to [q], work top braid, sew into central ball, turn, roll back along work. Fill in this small central section with whole stitch. Repeat for other side.

14 Begin rib for balls at [r], add in pairs to work the little joins. Sew out into completed braid.

Medallion

15 Begin rib for scrolls at [s], turn and fill in.

16 Rib round the inside of the oval, carry pairs into the whole stitch section.

17 Rib round and fill in inner and outer scallops.

18 Work the rib joining the two scrolls and the whole stitch loop.

Bells

An alternative way of working the bells would be to rib all the way round the outside.

19 Rib from [t] to [u], turn and fill in section [v] of the bell, leave pairs hanging.

20 Work clanger, then continue with the pairs that were left hanging and rib them round to sew out into the clanger. Work the other small section of rib.

21 Rib and fill bell. In this case there are alternate bands of whole stitch and pearl bars.

Bows and Bells, lower section

22 Work the two bell rings and chain.

23 Flowers and leaves. The flowers have the centres ribbed round. The pairs are used to fill the centre and carried on out into the petals.

Fillings

A Four Pin with Leadworks.
B Four Pin.
C No Pin.
D Pin and Stitch.
E Blossom.

Pricking 2b

Note 2

When pinning down work it is usually sufficient to press down and take out every other pin. If, however, pinholes are to be sewn into later, all the pins may be pushed down in order to keep the pinholes clear. Sometimes the outside edges of the work will loose their smooth curves if every other pin is removed. In this case too, all pins may be pushed down.

3 Butterfly Bush

Worked in Old 200 Thread

Butterfly Bush

Diagram 3

Pricking 3

Diagram 3a Four Pin Bud Leaf

Diagram 3b Whole and Half Stitch Leaf

Working Notes

Take care when pricking the holes for the circles – if the divisions between the scallops, i.e., the coarse crossings, are not at right angles to the edge, it may be necessary to alter the position of the pinholes slightly. Always cross the coarse from the outside of the scallop.

When working the leaves, try to organize the rows so that no back stitches are needed.

When working down towards a four pin bud, make sure the rows of weaving are horizontal and at right angles to the edges.

Six pairs are used for the main rib stems. Reduce to five pairs for the raised work and all tendrils. All the extra little tendrils and sepals round the leaves have to be carefully considered, to bring them into the completed leaf at a smooth angle.

There are several different patterns for the inner circle. (*See* Prickings 3a and b.)

Working Order

1 Begin by working the inner and outer circles, starting on a straight line at [a]. An extra pair was added for the whole stitch scallops and taken out for the half stitch.

2 Four pin bud leaves. Begin at [b] and work rib and leadwork centre, continue into rib stem and sew into the outer circle.

Start again at [b], rib up one side of the leaf, turn at the top and fill in, carry pairs onto the other side, rib up and fill in.

3 Whole and half stitch leaves. Begin at [c] by ribbing up the outer side of the leaf, turn and fill in. At the bottom carry pairs over into the other side of the leaf. Rib up to the top, turn and fill in. The two halves of the leaf are joined by swing leadworks.

4 No pin leaf. Begin at the tip of the rib at [d], work into the half stitch vein and out into the stem that first touches the inner circle. Continue round to sew out into the outer circle. Set up at [e], rib round both sides of the leaf and fill in with No Pin.

5 Butterfly.

Fillings

A Net.
B Spotted Net.
C No Pin.
D Four Pin.

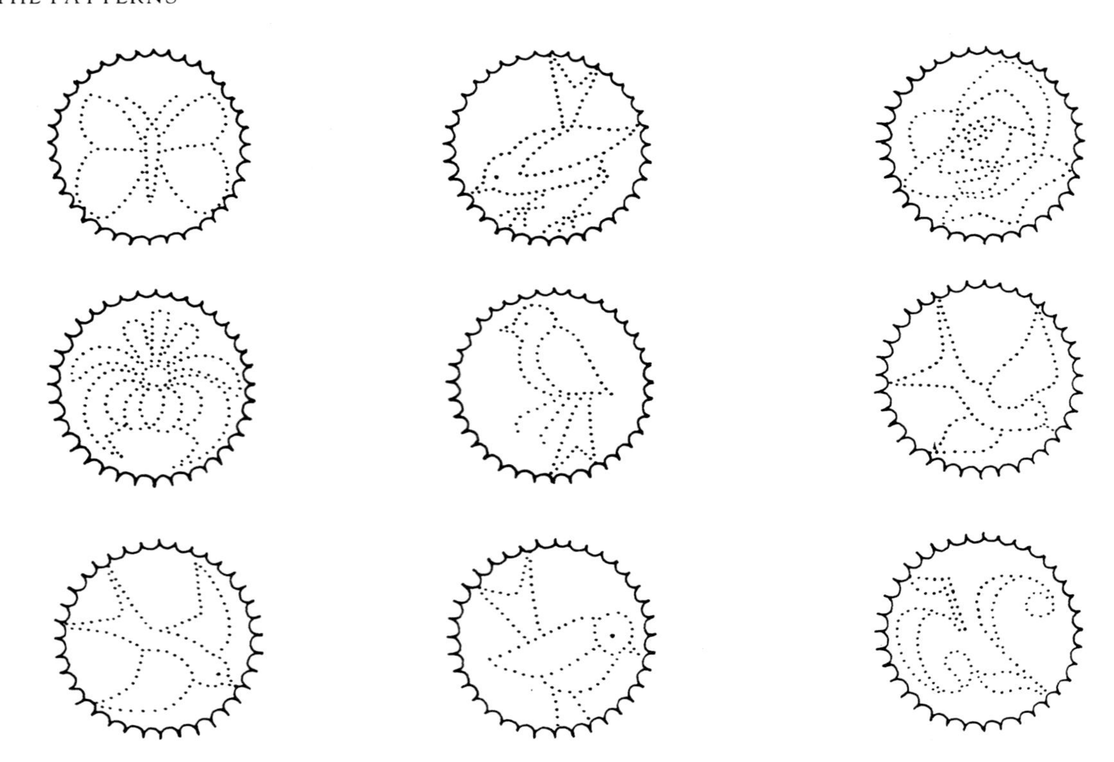

Pricking 3a Alternative Centres for Butterfly Bush

Pricking 3b

Note 3

A good edge with a firm smooth line is achieved by putting in edge pins slightly out and slightly back, pulling up firmly at the end of every row and having the right amount of pairs in the work, so that the pinholes do not drag. When going round a sharp bend, the runner pairs may be tied once after working through the coarse pair on the outer edge. This helps to keep the pinholes small and neat.

4 Tiny Bird

INTERPRETED BY SUSAN HANNAFORD HILL

Worked in Old 200 Thread

The tiny bird is an alternative centre for the Butterfly Bush (Pattern 3). The wing is ribbed from the outside tip, the tail sewn out into the wing, and the head and body started from the beak.

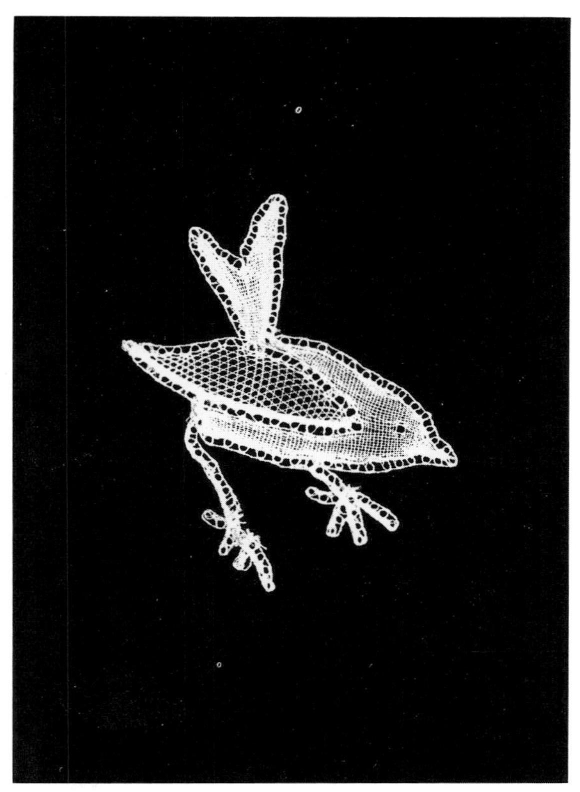

Tiny Bird

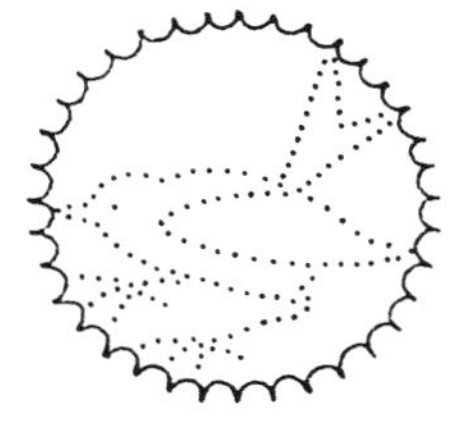

Pricking 4

Note 4

The number of pairs to use for any piece of work depends upon the thickness of the thread and the preference of the worker. While the work is getting wider, it is necessary to add more pairs; when it starts to narrow, pairs are taken out. If there are too many pairs in, the work will buckle and not lie flat; if there are not enough pairs in, the work will look sparse and pull away from the pinholes.

5 Butterfly Sampler

INTERPRETED BY PEGGY SNOWDON

Worked in 180 Thread

Working Notes

This pattern has several points and scrolls in the braid, both of which need special attention – it may be helpful to tie the runners once, after working through the coarse pair.

When there are more than three back stitches to be made round a point, it is advisable to alternate the back stitches with working the runners through to within the coarse pair, leaving them there, and working back with the last pair the runners passed through.

Butterfly Sampler

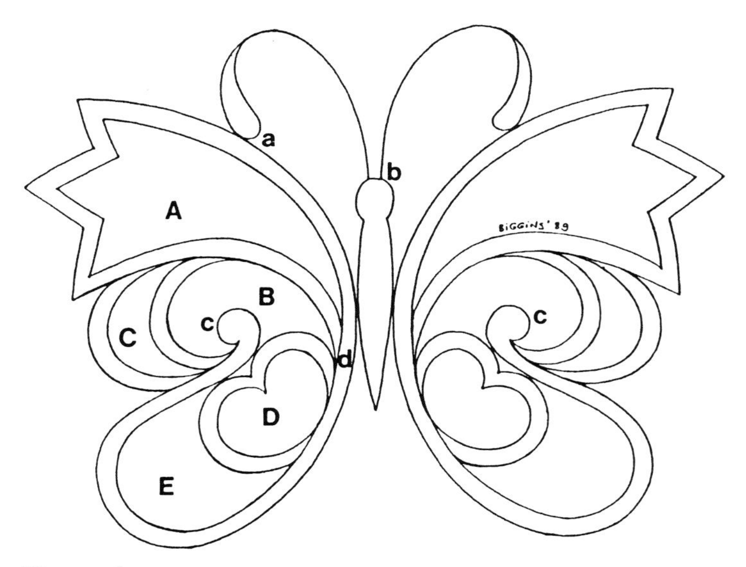

Diagram 5

Working Order

1 Body. Begin by working both antennae from [a] and joining them at the top of the head at [b], where a coarse pair is added. Remember to keep a pair laid back at the second hole from the bottom, to hold the tie back tassel.

2 The wings are begun from the scroll at [c] and sewn into the braid at [d]. The remaining braids can now be worked.

Pricking 5

Fillings

A Daisy.
B Whole Stitch Block Variation.
C Half Stitch.
D Taunton.
E Snowflake.

Note 5

When working a filling, sew out pairs as the filling progresses, but do not tie and cut off. Leave the pairs either until they are in the way or are needed for further use, then if a mistake occurs in the filling, the sewing can be undone and the mistake corrected.

6 Buttonhole Posy

INTERPRETED BY BERYL MAW

Worked in 180 Thread

Buttonhole Posy

Working Notes

The top flower and the petal flower pose several difficult problems.

The threads have not been rolled from one petal to another because the rib emphasizes the overlapping effect of the petals, but it would be possible to bunch up the threads and roll them up the side of the adjoining petal if this effect is required.

Merging the stems and leaves, instead of sewing pairs from one stem out into another, makes a smoother line.

The shading in of the petals of the top flower is achieved by gradually introducing whole stitches into the half stitch petal in the middle of the row.

Diagram 6

Working Order

Top Flower

1 Start at the top point at [a]. Where the braid widens out to the two points, as well as working out on a straight line, extra pairs can be added by hanging pairs onto temporary pins and cutting off the looped ends later. Leave the pairs hanging when the neck is reached.

2 Work both the scrolls from [b] and merge them with the pairs left hanging. Care is needed at this stage to keep the work straight. Divide the pairs in half to work down each side of the narrow braid. Work one side for a short way only, as far as [c] and finish off. Work the other side to meet the first braid and join the two braids at [c].

3 Starting at [d], rib round the centre petal and join to the braid. Rib all the other petals, sewing the rib into a petal and out into the braid. Keep bunches long as there will be further sewings into this braid. Fill all the petals with half stitch, graduating into whole stitch.

Open Flower

4 Rib pairs down the outside edge from [e], turn and work back to the top, crossing to the other side and working similarly. Rib round the small petals.

5 Begin the rib for the central leaf at [f], sew into the flower and use these pairs to work up one side of the leaf and down the other. Work the other two leaves the same way.

Petal Flower

6 Calyx. Hang up five pairs at [g], four pairs for the rib and one pair to leave behind. Work the tiny circle with four pairs and, on reaching the join, bring in the extra pair hung in at the beginning to make a neat join instead of a sewing. Work round to the

other tiny circle with these pairs. On reaching the circle at [h], lay a pair back out of the rib and continue the circle with four pairs. Join the circle and sew out. The laid back pair may be useful to hold the tie back tassel.

7 Petals. Rib round the central petal from [j] and sew out into the calyx rib. Sew rib pairs into the calyx rib for the two outer petals and sew out into the calyx. Rib along the top of the two remaining petals. Fill the petals with half stitch and sew out into the calyx rib, making tie back tassels and keeping bunches long, to keep the pinholes clear.

8 Rib the lower edge of the calyx, sewing into the petals at [k] and sewing out at [m]. Fill the calyx with whole stitch, working from the base.

Medallion

9 Work a whole stitch braid round the oval starting at [n]. Join and continue round the upper section. Join in the centre.

10 Work the scrolls from [p] and join to the braid.

11 Rib the small petals.

12 Stems and lower leaves. Hang pairs for the stems into the three flowers and merge them where they meet. The two lower leaves are started with a rib at [q]. Turn at the bottom and work up one side and down the other. The last part of the stem is worked using some of the downrights from the last leaf as runners, which are each sewn into the medallion.

Pricking 6

Fillings

A Whole Stitch Block Variation.
B Jubilee.
C No Pin.
D Toad in the Hole with Enclosed Pinholes.

Note 6

Where there are several sewings to be made into the same hole or more than one point of the pattern ends in the same place, keep the sewn in threads long so that they can be held back out of the way for further sewings. If the threads are cut off short, they may become unpicked when using the hole a second time.

7 Devon County Show 1989

Devon County Show 1989

This pattern was a set piece in the W.I. section of the Devon County Show. The interpretations shown were placed first, second and third.

Working Notes

This pattern was adapted from the Buttonhole Posy (Pattern 6) to make a simpler design. Even though the design is straightforward, each pattern is worked in a different way. Few instructions are given, as the direction of the threads can be seen from the photograph.

Working Order

1 First Pattern 180 Thread. Start with a rib round the flower centre, beginning at [a] and carry the threads on to rib around the central leaf. Add the stems of both flowers after the flowers are complete. Start the leaf stem with the top divided leaf at [f]. Merge each stem with the joining stems and work down to the bottom, ending the work with a tie back tassel at [b].

2 Second Pattern 120 Thread. Begin at the bottom of the stem at [b] and work up into

Devon County Show 1989, First, Beryl Maw

the central leaf of the top flower. Add the top piece of rib from [c] to [d] after the leaves have been worked. Hang the pairs for the stem of the open flower into the main stem at [e]. Cut out the coarse pair for the rib round the edge of the first petal, work back over the petal and carry rib pairs on into the second petal. Begin the leaf stem with the top divided leaf at [f].

3 Third Pattern 120 Thread. Begin the work at the bottom of the stem at [b] and use the pairs to work into the flower petals. Sew the open flower and leaves out into the main stem.

Fillings

A Leaf Flower – Daisy (small pricking *see* Filling 2).
Open Flower – Four Pin Flower and Leadworks.

B Leaf Flower – Pin and Stitch with Leadworks.
Open Flower – Toad in the Hole Variation.

C Leaf Flower – Pin and Chain.
Open Flower – Traffic Lights (Toad in the Hole Variation).

Diagram 7

Pricking 7

Note 7

Always support a sewing with a pin, i.e. replace the pin in the hole where the sewing has been taken. This will prevent the work from pulling out of shape round the edges when beginning or tying off.

Devon County Show 1989, Second, Sylvia Scarlett

Devon County Show 1989, Third, Dilys Hendy

8 Bowl of Roses

Worked in 180 Thread

Working Notes

This bowl of roses is worked in two colours. The four top roses and two buds are in white, and the bowl is worked in ecru.

It would be almost impossible to give instructions for this pattern, as *each* petal poses its own problems.

By referring to the photograph, it is possible to follow the directions of most of the threads. Before beginning each rose, make a tracing of it and work out your own flow chart, carrying threads on wherever possible.

The roses are worked in the order 1–6.

Begin each rose at [a].

Keep end tassels long so that they can be held back out of the way for further sewings. Keep all pinholes clear and firm, as nearly all of them have to be sewn into at least once.

The filling in the bowl is Four Pin Flower and Leadwork.

Bowl of Roses

Diagram 8

Pricking 8

Note 8

When beginning a piece of work, always spend some time deciding the best way to work it. If possible, there should always be a completed section into which to sew, to avoid ending with a tie back tassel at a point, or leaving pairs hanging unnecessarily.

9 Celebrations

Worked in 180 Thread

Working Notes

This pattern is easier to work if three separate prickings are made, so that each section can be worked on top of the pillow. Make one pricking of the whole pattern, and two separate prickings of the outside heart ovals. Work the two heart ovals first, then pin them onto the whole pricking and work the bird oval to join the two outside ovals.

There is a separate pricking of the two birds (Pricking 9a), as the original design was altered to make it easier to work.

Alternatively, a single pricking could be used and moved, but as it is so large, the card would tend to get too misshapen.

First finish all parts of the heart ovals, i.e. swags, heart, leaves and tendrils, as then the fillings can be started at the top and pairs carried right down, where appropriate, through the fillings, to the bottom.

When working the fillings of the second side section, especially the leaves, it is a mistake to try to get them to match the first section; treat each one as its own space and it will work more satisfactorily.

Celebrations

Celebrations, detail

Celebrations, detail

Pricking 9

Working Order

1 Start first oval at [a] to allow work to carry on into braid.

2 Work braid into second oval.

3 Carry threads from braid into second oval.

4 Sew pairs for bottom loops into braid and oval at [b]. Purls on the outside edge.

5 Start chain at [c], work round into chain [d], above oval [3] and work back to [c]. Sew out.

6 Half stitch edging around the heart, beginning at [e]. This is worked with seven pairs, including a coarse pair.

7 Fill in heart.

8 Start main rib stem at the top of the tendril at [f]. Add in pairs for the centre of the leaf. Work right round and attach to the chain at [d] and on into the divided leaf [g].

Diagram 9

9 Leaves. Refer to the close-up photograph and try to work out the best way of keeping all the joins as smooth as possible. Take all the tendrils down into the work so as not to end at a tendril tip.

10 Work outside half stitch whirl, beginning at the tip and sewing out into main rib.

11 Fillings. Sew in for net into the top rib, and carry pairs, where appropriate, on through to the bottom braid.

12 Fill in ovals and bottom loops.

Repeat for other side.
Lift the completed heart ovals and pin onto whole pricking.

13 Join the ovals from the completed sections with a braid, sewing in at [h].

14 Work bottom loops with purls.

15 Work chain from [d] to [j] and back.

16 Bird. Start body at beak and work to [k] where the pairs can be carried into the rib for the tail feathers.

17 Complete tail feathers.

18 Upper wing. Sew in pairs at [m], rib up to [n], turn and work over to [p]. Roll the pairs up the wing to [n] and rib on to the tip of the wing feather at [q]. Complete outer feathers.

19 Work other bird.

20 Work both braids for inner wings. Sew in braid at [r] and out into the opposite body.

21 Fill in inner wings with half stitch.

22 Half stitch frills on inner wings.

Pricking 9a

23 Flowers.

24 Fill in background, starting at the top and carrying pairs down.

25 Fill in bottom loops.

Fillings

A Toad in the Hole with Enclosed Pinholes.
B Italian.
C Strawberry backed with Half Stitch.
D Trolley Net.
E Traffic Lights.
F Blossom.
G Diamond with Leadworks.
H Devon Cutworks.
J Swing and Pin.
K Pin and Stitch.
L Four Pin.
M Taunton.

Note 9

When fitting a filling into a space, 'pretend' that the filling is going on over the edge. It is then easier to decide which holes the pairs should be sewn into, as the edge of a shape always causes the problem. Remember, when trying to decide if there is space for a pinhole in the filling, a crowd looks better than a gap.

10 Linked Hearts

Worked in 180 Thread

Working Notes

The Linked Heart design is taken from Celebrations (Pattern 9). It is worked with six pairs and a coarse pair. The scalloped braid is started at [a] and sewn out at [b]. Sew in again at [c] and out at [d].

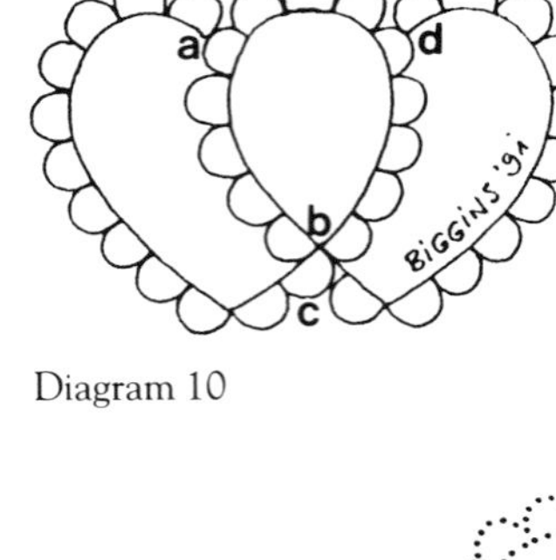

Diagram 10

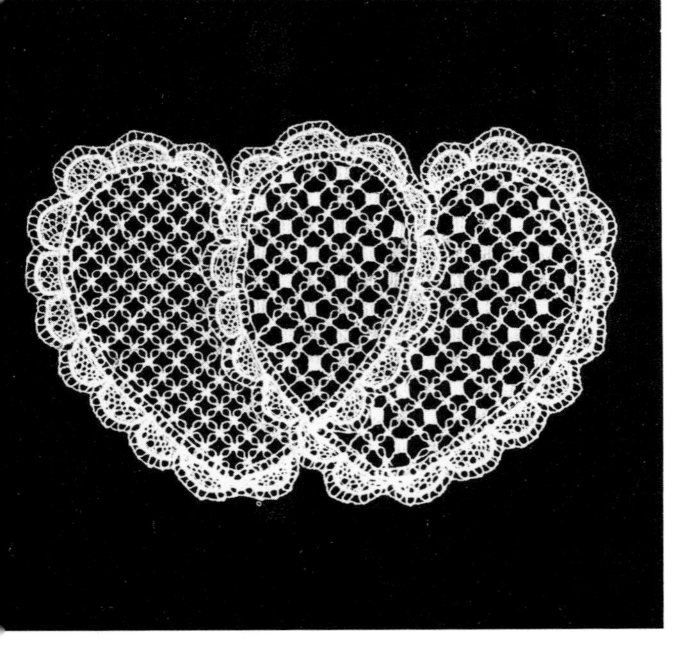
Linked Hearts

Pricking 10

Fillings

A Four Pin Flower and Leadwork (on a Four Pin grid).
B Daisy, pricked at every intersection on 1 mm graph paper (if Daisy filling is pricked on this size grid, it is only suitable for threads of 180 or over).

Note 10

Crossing two sets of pairs, which is done in fillings such as Jubilee, Snowflake and Daisy. Take the second pair from the left through the two pairs on the right in whole stitch, and leave. Take the left hand pair through the two middle pairs in whole stitch. The two pairs have now crossed through each other.

When Daisy is pricked very small, i.e. on every intersection on 1 mm graph paper, use each of the four pairs as one bobbin and make a whole stitch with them. This makes a smaller crossing.

11 Chrysanthemums

Worked in 120 and 200 Thread

Chrysanthemums

Chrysanthemums

Chrysanthemums

Working Notes

Originally this pattern was a City and Guilds project, working the same pattern in different sizes and using different thicknesses of thread. The small pattern was worked first in 200 thread, but was definitely too fussy. The larger pattern is a mirror image and the bottom leaves are simplified. It is an example of how a pattern can be altered, either to make it easier to work, or more pleasing to the eye.

The leaf veins in the large pattern are half stitch braids and in the small pattern they are divided ribs with leadworks.

Diagram 11

Working Order

1 Flowers. Set up rib pairs for the centre at [a], rib round the central ring and join at [a]. Work back over, carrying rib pairs on into the top edge of the large serrated petal [b]. These pairs can be carried on to rib into the lowest petal [c].

Work the two lower petals on the other side the same, sewing in rib pairs at [a].

Sew in rib pairs at [d] and rib and roll all the seven top petals.

2 The Large Leaf. Each section is worked separately. Set up for the central vein at [e] and sew it out into the flower. Set up again at [f], divide at [e] and work down either side of the vein. Do the same with the two sections from [g] and [h]. The two bottom sections have a central rib vein attached at the bottom, and the pairs are then continued on around the leaf.

3 Begin bud at [j] with rib pairs, work into the braid and when complete, use the pairs to turn into the outer petals [k]. Set up again at [m] for the other side petals.

Fillings

A Trolley Net B Italian	large pattern
A No Pin B Swing and Pin	small pattern

Pricking 11

Pricking 11a

Note 11

Try not to use a crochet hook, however fine, for difficult sewings. Use an inverted beading needle threaded with a length of lace thread. Insert this into the hole and then remove it, leaving a loop of thread through which to pass the bobbin. By holding on to the beading needle and the other end of the length of thread, the bobbin being sewn can be pulled through. Remove the loose length of thread and pass the other bobbin of the pair to be sewn in through the loop. This prevents the edges of the pinhole being caught and torn or broken.

12 Cornucopia

INTERPRETED BY SYLVIA SCARLETT

Worked in 170 Egyptian Gassed Cotton

Working Notes

The heart-shaped leaves and the divided leaves on the main stem have all been finished at the tip, which is unusual, but adds to the many different ways of working leaves, which feature so largely in Honiton lace.

Cornucopia

Diagram 12

Working Order

1 Work around cross pieces. Fill with swing leadworks.

2 Begin centre strip at [a] and sew out into cross piece.

3 Sew rib pairs into cross piece and rib into point [a]. Turn and work back, sewing into cross piece. Work the other side the same.

4 Work the joining strip between the cross pieces. In this case they have been worked in alternate strips of half stitch and whole stitch with a twist vein.

5 Sew in rib pairs at [b] and work the tap leaves around the horn.

6 Sew in the braids for the hearts at the base of the horn at [a].

7 Heart-shaped leaves. Start at the tip at [c], rib round one section and roll up the centre and into the second section. Sew out into the start and make a tie back tassel. Fill these leaves with leadwork variations, backed with half stitch.

8 Two centre flowers.

9 Sew rib pairs into flower 8 at [d] and work right round into top divided leaf [e]. Turn at the top and work down one side and up the other, ending with a tie back tassel.

10 Work the rest of the leaves on the stem in the same way.

Pricking 12

11 Sew in rib for tap leaf at [f]. Rib and roll both sides.

12 The flowers have purls round the outside edge.

13 Scalloped leaves. Begin inner rib at [g] and rib round either side, join ribs at [h] and work down to sew into main stem. Work rib around the scallops and sew into inner rib, turn and work back over, alternating petals with half stitch and whole stitch, with one twist.

Fillings

A Toad in the Hole with Enclosed Pinholes.
B Italian.
C No Pin.
D Strawberry backed with Half Stitch.
E Devon Cutwork backed with Half Stitch.

Note 12

If a leadwork collapses at the bottom in a filling, such as Toad in the Hole, correct it straight away, otherwise it will spoil the whole filling. Usually, undoing the bottom of the leadwork and working two extra rows will do the trick, or put an extra one or two twists on the pair as they go in and come out of the leadwork.

13 Devon County Show 1990

Devon County Show 1990

Devon County Show 1990, First, Sylvia Scarlett (See also pp. 125 and 138)

This design was a set piece for the W.I. in one of the Lace Classes in the Devon County Show. The three pieces shown were placed first, second and third.

Working Notes

First pattern

Purl and leadwork edging taken from old lace. Work half stitch scallops before adding the purl edge. Work the purl edging with four pairs in the purl rib and one extra pair on the scallop side, used as the second pair for the leadwork and attached to each hole on the scallop side as the work progresses. The flower petals are whole stitch with windows.

Second pattern

Outer bars – half stitch vein. Inner bars – Chudleigh Twist (*see* Note 23).

Flower. Work central ring in rib, continue rib into petals, working the whole outline of the flower. Join to first petal and carry these threads on to work round with the half stitch backing (rather than working each petal down from top to bottom).

Third pattern

Unusual use of vein and holes in the outer bar and scallops. Four Pin used as background.

Working Order

1 Work the four little crescent shapes, starting at one of the points either with a rib, turning at the tip and working back, or flat work with a tie back tassel.

2 Work the four bars joining the crescents.

3 The scalloped edging and the top and bottom hoops can be worked continuously, beginning at [a] and sewing out into the start.

4 The flower may be worked first and the stem added afterwards, or sew in pairs for the stem at [b] and work straight up into the flower.

5 Stem (if not already worked).

6 Divided leaves.

The first piece is worked in a different order. Begin a rib at the top of braid 2. Rib down to the bottom of the braid and work back over to the top. Take the bunch of threads and roll them down the side of the completed braid to the bottom. At the bottom, carry these threads into the rib of the inner braid and repeat as for the first braid. On reaching the crescent shape at the top, work into this, adding a coarse pair and carry on into the scallops and down into the bottom crescent. Sew out into the inner braid.

Diagram 13

Pricking 13

Fillings

A Flower centre – Devon Cutwork.
Crescents – Margaret Maidment's, Four Pin Blocks.
Flower background – Trolley Net.
Top and bottom hoops – Snowflake.

B Flower centre – Cushion.
Crescents – Toad in the Hole with Enclosed Pins.
Flower background – Trolley Net.
Top and bottom hoops – Four Pin with Leadworks.

C Flower centre – Swing and Pin.
Crescents – Traffic Lights. (Toad-in-the-Hole Variation)
Flower background – Four Pin.
Top hoop – Whole Stitch Block Variation.
Bottom hoop – Blossom.

Note 13

Tension is probably the most important technique of all in the making of good lace. At the end of every row put the pin in slightly out and slightly back; hold the runner pair in one hand and straighten all the downright bobbins, pulling them gently but firmly into place in the direction in which they are travelling in the lace.

14 Fan

INTERPRETED BY JUNE GOLLAN

Worked in 180 Thread

Working Notes

Each fan leaf should be designed for its own sticks. This design is for a large fan, with a fairly shallow leaf. The two sides of the pattern in the drawing are different, giving an alternative arrangement. Make a tracing of one half of the design and reverse it so a mirror image is obtained. Parts of it could be taken out and rearranged for a different shaped fan leaf.

The design differs considerably from the photographed work, illustrating how the pattern can be adapted to suit the individual.

Fan

Diagram 14

Pricking 14

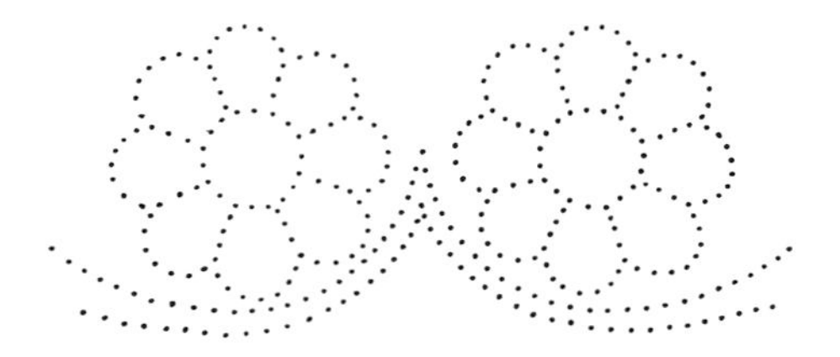

Pricking 14a

Working Order

1 Work the central braid continuously from the top scroll at [a], ending with a tie back tassel on the opposite top scroll at [b] (*see* Pricking 14). The vein is a half stitch vein, worked in the widest part of the braid (*see* Note 14). Sew in rib pairs for the tap leaves at [c]. Rib and roll all the leaves down to the bottom.

2 The daisies have a ribbed centre which is joined. The rib is carried on to outline the petals. Keep these pairs and add others to work over the top in one row whole stitch and one row half stitch.

3 The two divided leaves below the tap leaves are begun at the tip and divided in two where the central vein begins. Work each side down separately to sew into the braid. The centre is alternately leadwork and cross overs.

4 Tendrils.

Pricking 14b

Pricking 14c

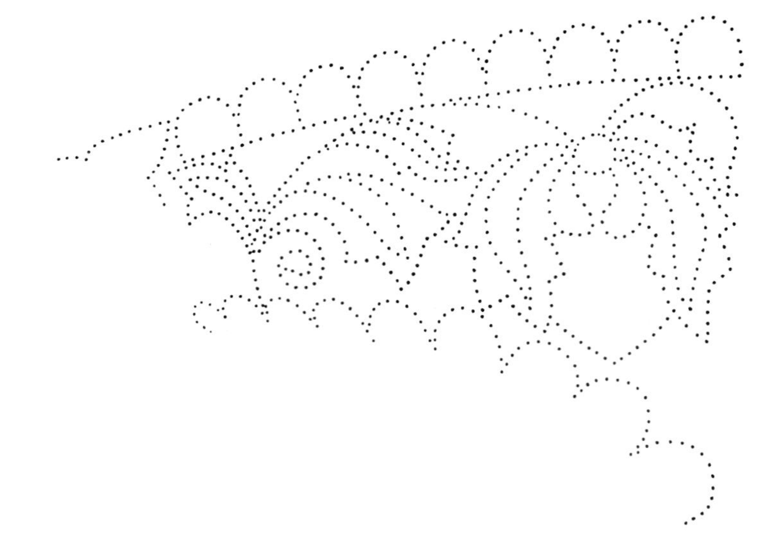

Pricking 14d

5 Hanging flower. Rib round the little circle, make a leadwork in the centre and use the rib pairs to back the circle with half stitch. Keep the sewn out pairs long. The divided leaves are sewn out into the circle, as are the little buds.

Diagram 14a

Fillings

The filling is Toad in the Hole

Note 14

Half stitch vein. Sort out one pair in the middle, or wherever the vein is to be. Put a pin either side of this pair, or note the bobbins on either side of the vein pair. Work through to the vein pair, twist the runners once and make a half stitch with the runners and the vein pair. Work on with the two leading bobbins and replace the pins either side of the other pair used to make the half stitch. Work on to the end of the row in whole stitch and repeat for each row.

15 Floral Edging

INTERPRETED BY CHRISTINE HAWKEN

Worked in 170/2 Gassed Egyptian Cotton

Floral Edging

Floral Edging, detail

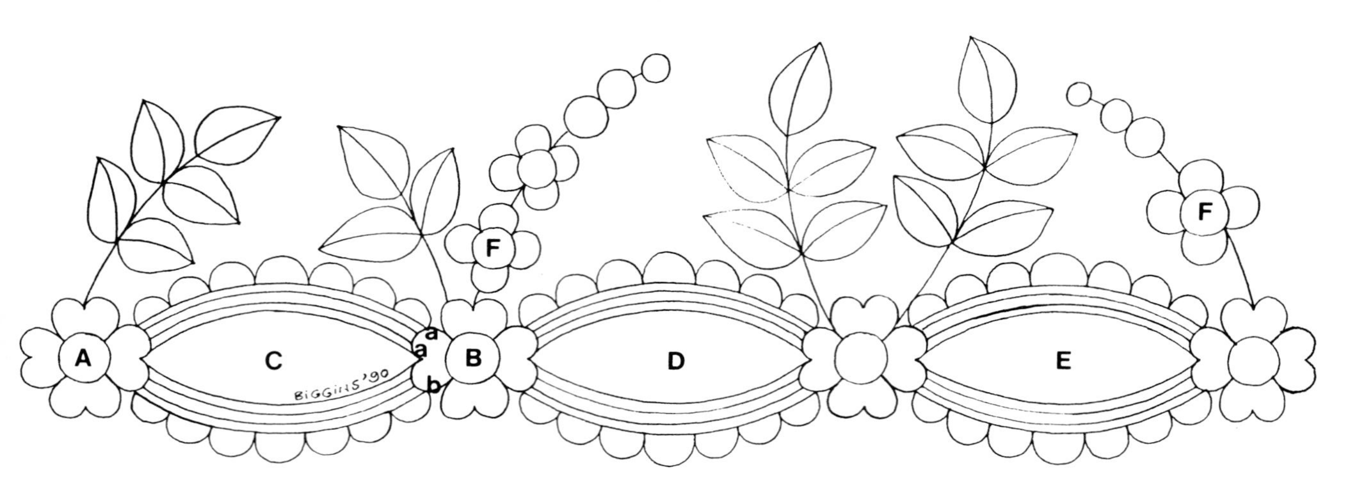

Diagram 15

Pricking 15

Working Notes

To vary this simple edging, leave out the sprays of leaves and flowers, or add more on the opposite side, to make a central panel for a christening gown.

The snatch pin braid (*see* Note 15) enclosing the filling makes a very light and pretty edging. The flower centres and leaf veins can all be varied.

Working Order

1 Work the flowers.

2 Sew pairs into the flowers at [a] and work snatch pin braid.

3 Sew in pairs for the scalloped edging at [b]. Work pearls on the outside edge.

4 Leaves and flower sprays.

Fillings

A Cartwheel.
B Diamond.
C Leadwork and Lattice.
D Brick.
E Leadworks with pinhole.
F No Pin.

Note 15

Snatch pin braid. For this braid, use one coarse pair. Sew in pairs for each side of the braid, hang the coarse pair up on a pin and bring the threads down in the fifth position from the outer edges on both sides. Now work both sides at the same time. *Work a whole stitch and three twists with both sets of edge pairs. Take the runners to the middle, twist seven times and put in a pin, return to the outside edge. Make up the edge stitch. Repeat for a second pinhole in the middle. Take the runners to the middle, twist runner pair three times, and use it with the pair from the other side to make a snatch leadwork. Twist both runners three times and return them to the outside edge. Repeat from *

N.B. A snatch pin braid may be worked with only one snatch pin between the leadworks.

16 Flower Bower

Interpreted by Yvonne Watts
and Dedicated to the Memory of Alan Watts

Worked in 180 Thread

Flower Bower, detail (See also frontispiece)

Pricking 16

E
12
12
t
t
s
r
k
7
D
9
11
m
8
F
C
G
p
n
10
13
13
q
u
u
B
v
14
v
4
BIGGINS '90
2
b
a
3
A
1
5
c
d
e
f
g
h
j
6

Diagram 16

Working Notes

The photographed work of the Flower Bower and the original design differ considerably, making this is a very clear example of how the patterns in this book are intended to be used. Many of the extra twirls can be left out if they are considered too fussy. The two side leaves [13], in particular, are open to individual interpretation, both examples being worked in an entirely different order.

Working Order

The Vase

1 Begin the rib at [a]. Work towards the outside edge, all around the base as far as [b]. Leave these pairs hanging. Rib round the centre section, then each of the sections individually, sewing out the first rib when the adjoining section has been worked.

2 Rib across the frill, catching pairs where they cross the rib.

3 Work the diamond filling and back the whole vase with half stitch from left to right.

4 Work the ball and joining ribs and scrolls. These can be worked in a variety of different ways.

Vase Stem

5 Begin at [c] and work up to sew out into the base of the vase. Add each of the other six sections from [d] – [j].

6 Hang rib pairs into side of section [j]. Rib and roll bottom shell.

Flowers

7 Begin the small flowers with a braid at [k], reduce to a rib and join at [k]. Carry these rib pairs out into the petals. The rib pairs are used to carry on and back the petals with half stitch.

8 Rib from [m] round the top of the centre, join the rib and carry these pairs out into the top row of the petals. Raise each of these ten petals and carry the pairs on to rib round the three lower petals. After ribbing the last petal, the pairs can be carried on into the inner rib. Fill these lower petals. Rib and fill the inner petals.

9 Sew rib pairs for these buds into flower [8]. Rib and roll the tap leaves to suit the pattern.

10 Rib round the centre from [n], join the rib and carry the pairs on into the lower petals. Sew in rib for upper petals at [p]. Work round centre petal and out to one side. Sew in another set of rib pairs at [p] and make a roll with these up the side of the completed centre petal. Work out to the other side. Back with whole stitch.

For the inner petals, hang rib pairs in at [q], rib and fill centre petal. Use the rib pairs to raise one set of side petals and some of the pairs used for the half stitch filling to raise the other side set of petals.

11 Rib round the centre from [r], carry pairs on to outline the lower petals. Rib and roll the top petals from [s]. Back with half stitch.

12 Top leaves. Work the centre vein first. Work the side taps from [t] and add the top leaf when the side taps are complete.

13 The working of these leaves is left to the discretion of the lacemaker, as each one is worked differently. But in both cases the rib begins from the centre at [u].

14 The buds begin from the tips of the leaves at [v] and sew out into leaves [13].

Flower Bower, detail

Fillings

A Diamond backed with Half Stitch.
B Four Pin Flower and Leadworks.
C Blossom.
D Double Blossom.
E No Pin.
F Pin and Stitch.
G Pin and Stitch with Leadworks.

Note 16

An alternative way of working Four Pin buds. In leaves [12] of the Flower Bower, the Four Pin buds show the bottom hole enclosed with a whole stitch. A whole stitch may also be worked with the two central pairs before setting pin 1 of the bud.

17 Formal Flower Pot

INTERPRETED BY SYLVIA SCARLETT

Worked in 140 Thread

Formal Flower Pot

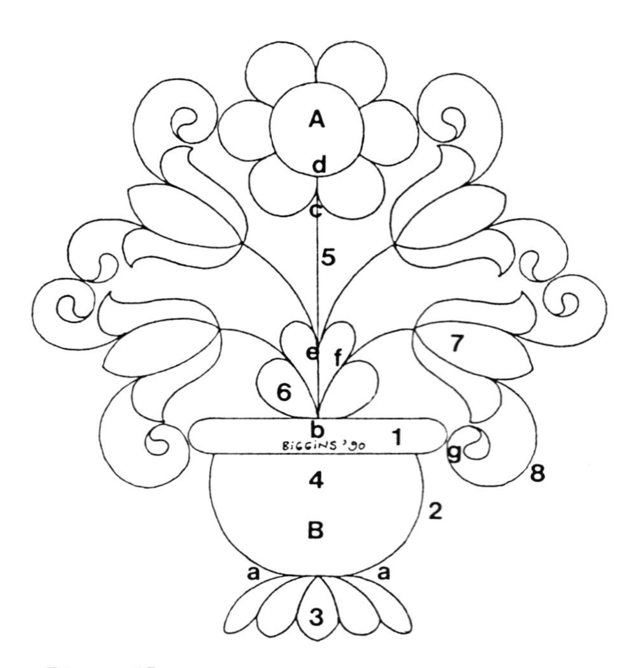

Diagram 17

Pricking 17

Working Notes

This pattern would be suitable for beginners to raised and rolled work.

Working Order

1 Begin with pot rim.

2 Rib round pot.

3 The pot stand. Work the two outer sections on both sides first, sew in rib pairs at [a] and add the central section last (to get the two sides of rib and roll to match). Some of these pairs can be carried on for the filling.

4 Fill in the flower pot.

5 Sew into the pot for the main flower stem at [b]. When the flower [c] is reached, make a straight line start from [c] to [d] for working into the petals. Work round the flower. (Optional Extra: when sewing out petals, save five pairs on the innermost edge of the completed flower at [d] and roll them round the inner edge of the flower.)

6 Hang in rib pairs at [e] and rib and roll central leaves.

7 Sew rib pairs into central leaves at [f] and work into the buds.

8 Tendrils. Begin at the tip [g] with pinholes on either side. Reduce to rib pairs and sew out into the bud.

Fillings

A Leadwork and Pinhole.
B Whole Stitch Block Variation.

Note 17

The distance between pinholes depends upon the thickness of thread being used. If the pinholes are uneven, badly pricked, or too far apart, alter them as they come to be used.

18 Flower Fountain

INTERPRETED BY SUSAN BRADSHAW

Worked in 170 Thread

Flower Fountain, detail (See also p. 6)

Diagram 18

Working Notes

The flowers in the bouquet are worked to give as much variety as possible. The flowers could be traced and rearranged.

The Whole Stitch Block filling in the small group of flowers [19] is very effective, as is the Swing and Pin variation backed with half stitch in the lower petals of flower [14]. The use of the one twist vein in flower [11] is a very interesting way of breaking up whole stitch.

The cornucopia is lettered [a]–[k], the flowers are lettered [a]–[w].

Working Order

Cornucopia

1 Set up the scroll at [1]. Cross the coarse at [a] and again at [b]. Work the two halves of the next section separately, working section [c] first. Work almost to the first spiral. Hang pairs into the side of section [c] for the spiral. Hang in extra pairs to work section [d], sew both sides out into the spiral.

Hang in pairs at [e] to work the first two spurs, sew out the spiral pairs into the completed spur. Fill in all the little half stitch sections as work progresses.

On the first spur at [f], hang in pairs to make the second spiral. Just past [g], sew in rib pairs for the end spur and work this spur so that the spiral pairs can be sewn out, into it. Roll and rib the remaining spurs. The top row of spurs is begun at [h], work this outer spur first. Sew rib pairs into the completed spur for the other two spurs. Rib round the top of these two spurs, turn and work back over them in whole stitch.

2 Rib the underside of the top of the cornucopia from [j] to [k], also the three central ribs. Work the rim in whole stitch.

3 Half stitch frill round the edge of the cornucopia. On the inner edge, the pairs can be carried on into the raised and rolled leaf [4].

4 Raised and rolled leaf.

5 Start at the tip of this leaf with eight pairs and a coarse pair. These pairs are divided into three, to make a neat tip to the leaf. Use the central bobbins to work the vein first, which is sewn out into the cornucopia. The two sides will need a coarse pair each and extra bobbins added quickly. Carry the pairs on into the raised taps. Work all the other leaves and tendrils.

Flowers

6 Begin the rib for flower [6] at [a]. Take the rib through the flower, down the stem and through the centre of flower [7]. Add a coarse pair for petal [b]. Carry pairs on in rib into [c] and [d], before ribbing down to sew into the rim of the cornucopia. Complete flower [6].

7 Sew rib pairs for flower [7] into petal [c] and rib and roll the petals. Ladder trails are worked in these petals.

8 Flower [8] is begun at the tip of the tendril [e] and worked to match flower [6].

9 Sew pairs for the leaves into the cornucopia rim at [f]. Rib and roll these four leaves.

10 Set up rib pairs at [g] and raise the three central petals. Alternatively, the centre ring could be ribbed round first. From the three central petals, carry the pairs out into the middle tier. The outer petals are worked with one raised edge and two half stitch veins in each petal (*see* Note 14).

11 Set up rib pairs at [h]. Join the rib and use the pairs to work back over the centre. These pairs can be carried on into the rib of petal [j]. The pairs can be carried on, in a roll, where appropriate. The central petal and petals [k] and [m] are worked flat. The three top petals are worked last. Sew the rib pairs into petal [k].

12 Start the calyx at [n], adding quickly to fill out the work where it widens. Cross the coarse thread at the bottom and change to half stitch. Sew the rib stem out into flower [11]. Work the divided leaves.

For the petals, sew rib pairs into the calyx at [p], rib and roll the first four petals, hanging in a coarse pair for the whole stitch braid, at the top of each petal. Sew the rib out into the centre, after working the fourth petal. Set up again at [q] and rib and roll petals into the centre. After working the braid across the top petal, roll the pairs down to sew out into the centre, so that both sides match. The Pin and Chain filling is pricked to create a fan effect.

13 Set up at [r] and work centre petal. Carry rib pairs on into two side raised petals, [s] and [t]. These pairs carry on to rib round the two lower open petals. Work the centre whole stitch section by sewing into petal [s], working around the central petal and sewing out into [t]. Sew rib pairs into one of the lower open petals and work the outer row.

14 Set up rib pairs for the underside of the centre at [u]. The petals can all be worked continuously.

Diagram 18a

Pricking 18

The bottom, inner row of petals is ribbed and the rib pairs carried on into the upper whole stitch petals. The lowest half stitch petals are ribbed with a variation of Swing and Pin filling, and backed with half stitch. The half stitch backing is worked across the whole of the centre.

15 Begin at [v] and work down to rib into tiny circle. Use these pairs to rib into the two side leaves.

Work the centre half stitch section round the central leaf, from one lower leaf to the other. Rib round the central large petal and sew out. Sew rib pairs into either side of the central petal and rib both sets of side petals.

16 Leaves. Hang rib pairs up at [w] and work through the middle of the first divided leaf. Attach to flower [14] and turn. Work all the divided leaves.

17 Flower [17] is begun at the tip of one of the tendrils and worked to match [6] and [8].

18 The top group of small flowers has a ribbed centre, which carries on into the half stitch petals.

19 The other small flowers have a ribbed and backed centre, which carries on into the rib petals. The fillings are variations of Whole Stitch Blocks.

Fillings

A Daisy.
B Italian.
C Pin and Stitch with Leadworks.
D Devon Cutworks.
E Pin and Chain.

Flower Fountain, detail

Note 18

Leadworks will not collapse if they are exactly the right size for the space intended. As a general rule, make the leadwork the size needed, then add two extra rows. If it still collapses, an extra one or two twists on the pairs before and after the leadwork should help.

19 Horseshoe Spray

Worked in 180 Thread

Horseshoe Spray

Horseshoe Spray, upper sections

Working Notes

This pattern has much scope for individual interpretation. The original drawing differs slightly from the pricking, as the circles in the horseshoe are not worked and the divisions in the leaves have been left out, as they would make the drawing and pricking even more cluttered and complicated.

By looking at the photographs, it can be seen that the leaves can be broken up in different ways to make more manageable areas.

As the pattern is too large to be worked in one piece, the lace should be moved three times so that the part of the work in progress can always be worked on the top of the pillow.

Work Section One, carefully lift the lace off the pricking so that Section Two is central on the top of the pillow, re-pin Section One. When both Sections One and Two are completed, lift both off and position Section Three on pillow centre. Re-pin One and Two.

Horseshoe Spray, detail

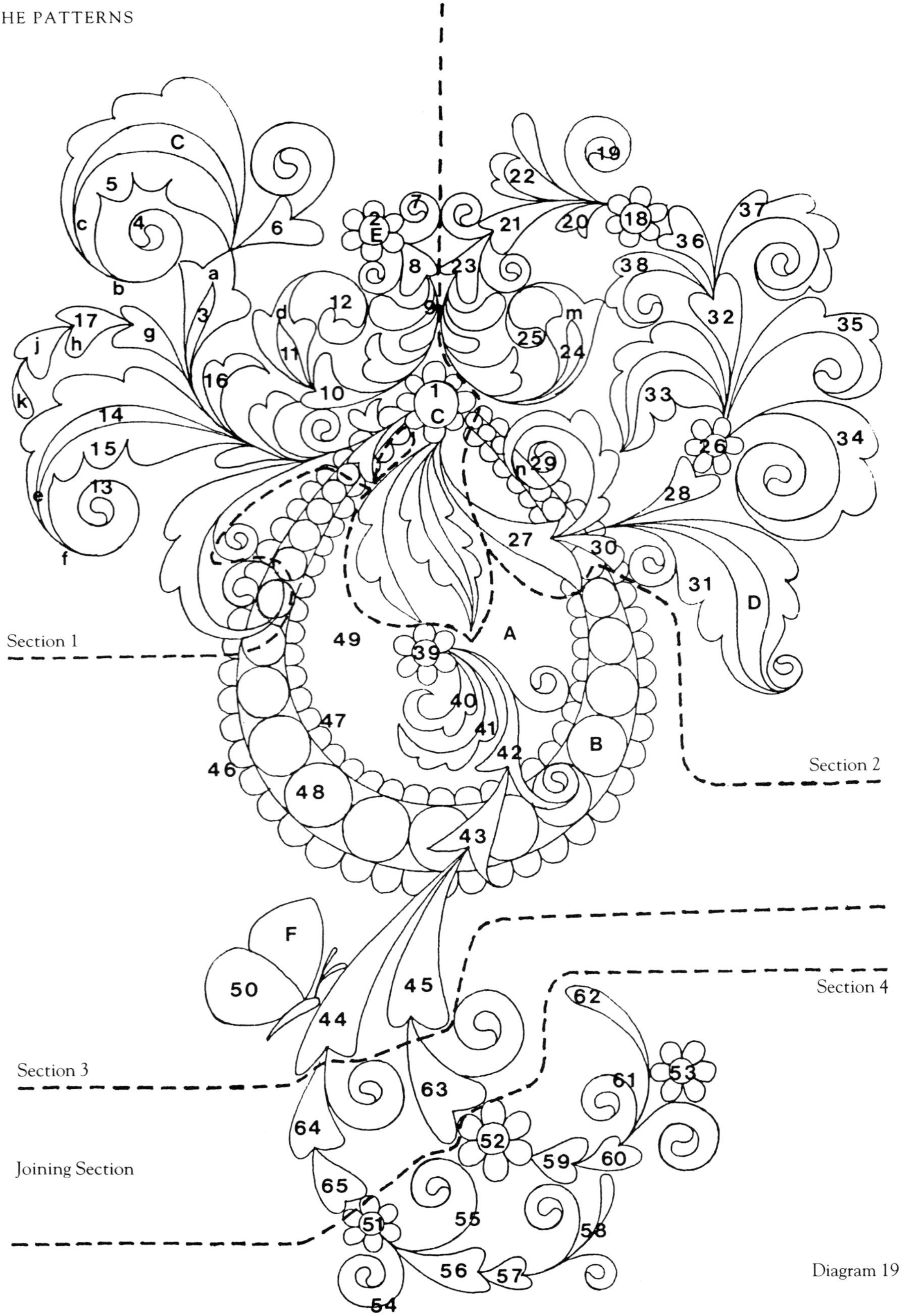

Section 1

Section 2

Section 4

Section 3

Joining Section

Diagram 19

The last section, Section Four, is worked separately on another pillow. When this has been worked, re-pin the two long leaves below the horseshoe, and work the three leaves and two tendrils joining the two sections.

One of the interesting problems in this piece is to get the fillings to curve round evenly in the leaves.

Working Order

Section One

1 Work the central flower.

2 Flower.

3 Begin vein at [a], work into rib and sew into flower [1].

4 Begin tendril, work rib round the outside of the top leaf to where the edge of the leaf dips in. The pinholes are then on the inside of the curve. Backstitch on each of the three holes [a], [b] and [c] (*see* Diagram 19a) to get the rib to lie flat. At the tip of leaf [3], add a coarse pair and work leaf.

5 Hang pairs into the rib at [b], adding one coarse bobbin and one more bobbin on the side without the rib. Divide the leaf at [c] and work down to the bottom. Pairs from the underside of the leaf can be carried onto leaf [6].

6 Work leaf [6].

7 Tendril. Sew out into flower [2]. Keep pairs for leaf [8].

8 Carry pairs from tendril [7] into leaf [8].

9 Sew pairs for rib into leaf [8]. Rib up into leaf [10].

10 Work leaf [10].

11 Set up at [d] and work vein.

12 Tendril. Add a coarse pair where the leaf widens and work leaf [11], dividing the braid at [d].

13 Tendril. Work into rib round top edge of the leaf and sew out into rib, below leaf [3].

14 Set up vein at [e]; both sides are ribbed separately and the leadworks added afterwards. Sew out into rib.

15 Hang pairs into rib [13] at [f], plus one coarse bobbin and one more bobbin on the side without the rib, and work the leaf, dividing the pairs where the vein begins at [e]. The pairs from the underside of the leaf can be carried on into leaf [16].

16 Work leaf [16].

17 Work this sequence of leaves [g], [h], [j], [k], finishing each onto the previous section worked. All the extra leaves and tendrils can now be worked.

Lift this completed section carefully, do not turn it over or it will be more difficult to replace the pins exactly. Move the pricking so that Section Two is in the centre of the pillow and re-pin Section One. The work to be joined should be pinned very securely, but the rest of the work can be pinned down just to hold it in place.

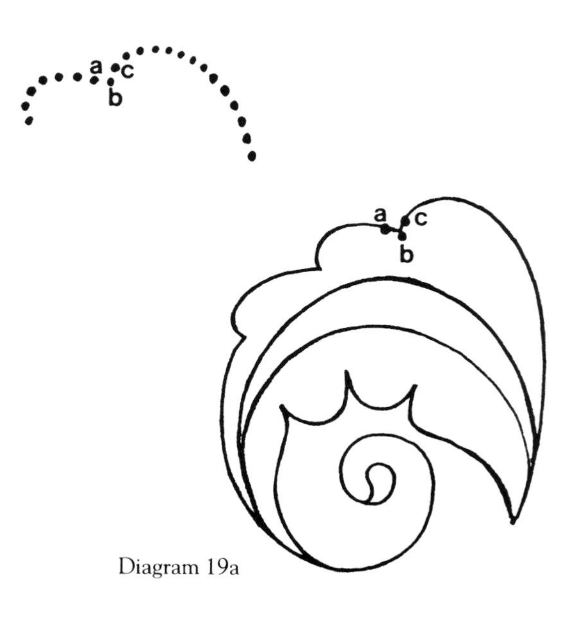

Diagram 19a

Section Two

18 Flower.

19 Work tendril, sew into flower and carry pairs on into rib for leaf [20].

20 Work leaf [20].

21 Sew into leaf [20]. Work leaf.

22 Work the two leaves attached to leaf [21].

23 Sew pairs into leaf [21]. Work leaf.

24 Set up at [m]. Work leaf vein and on into rib, sewing out into leaf [23].

25 Work tendril, add in pairs where leaf widens and sew out into the vein. Now all the other leaves and tendrils on this stem can be worked.

26 Flower.

Pricking 19

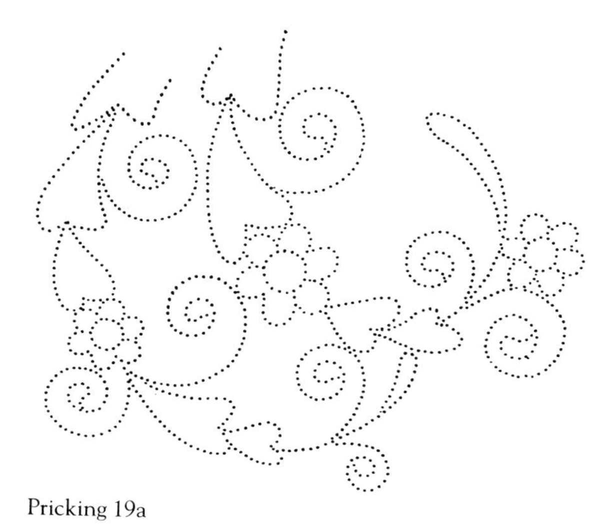

Pricking 19a

27 Sew pairs into central flower [1]. Work leaf.

28 Sew pairs into leaf [27] and rib up into leaf [28].

29 Begin leaf at the tip of the tendril and rib down the outer side. Sew out into stem [28]. Sew pairs into the rib at the top of the leaf where it widens at [n]. Add coarse thread and one more bobbin for inner edge and work down leaf, carrying pairs on into leaf [30].

30 Leaf.

31 Work this leaf similar to leaf [5].

32 Work leaves in sequence [32]–[38].

Lift these two completed sections and reposition the pricking so that Section Three is on the middle of the pillow. Re-pin work especially firmly where it is to be joined.

Section Three

39 Flower.

40 Work leaves in sequence [40]–[45]

46 & 47 The outer and inner braids of the horseshoe. Work over the top of the already completed scrolls and leaves, unless the distance is too great, in which case sew pairs out and sew them in again, e.g. for leaves 27 and 30.

48 & 49 Fillings.

50 Butterfly. Use four pairs for each antennae. Where they join, take out two downright pairs.

This completes the whole of the top section. Now work the bottom small Section Four on another pillow, following the sequence from 51–62. Rib 54 can be sewn into the flower and carried on into rib 55. End at the tip.

Lift the whole of the top three sections and pin down the two bottom leaves, 44 and 45. Take care to protect the unsupported work.

63, 64 & 65 Work, joining leaves and tendrils.

Fillings

A Diamond.
B Toad in the Hole with Enclosed Pins.
C Swing and Pin.
D Devon Cutworks.
E No Pin.
F Snowflake.

Note 19

Moving work. Sometimes, when making large pieces of lace, work has to be moved to enable the work in progress to lie on the top of the pillow. In such a case, finish a section, cut off all the bobbins, and carefully take out all the pins. Do not lift the lace as it will be difficult to replace the pins in the correct holes. Lift the pricking and the completed lace and reposition the next section to be worked on the top of the pillow. Re-pin the completed section of lace where the work is to be joined very securely.

20 Ice Cream Cornucopia

Worked in 180 Thread

Ice Cream Cornucopia

Diagram 20

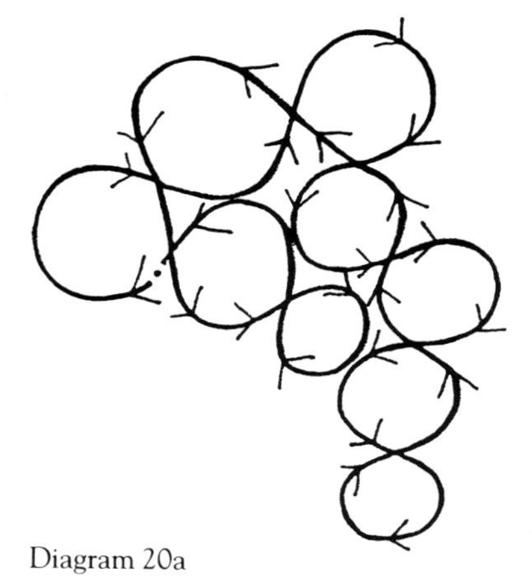

Diagram 20a

Working Notes

The main problem with this design is the number of sewings into the rib where the leaves join the oranges. Remember to leave the sewn-in ends long, to hold back out of the way for further sewings.

The open filling (Whole Stitch Block Variation) has probably worked more successfully than the closer No Pin, as it provides more of a contrast with the grapes.

Pairs can be left sewn out and carried over into other sections at many points in the pattern.

Working Order

1 Begin the rib for the cornucopia at [a] by working it like a chain, zig-zagging the rib down to the bottom, except for the tip, which is added afterwards, and ribbing and rolling back up to [a].

2 Fill in each section with half stitch separately.

3 Work the little flowers in the oranges.

4 Rib round the whole orange beginning at [b] and carry pairs on into the second orange.

5 Fill the oranges.

6 Work the grapes in one continuous rib from [c], taking care to keep changing the pinholes to the outside curve of the rib.

7 Fill grapes.

8 Work leaves. Add the leadworks in the centres of the leaves afterwards.

Fillings

A Whole Stitch Block Variation.
B No Pin.
C Swing and Stitch.

Pricking 20

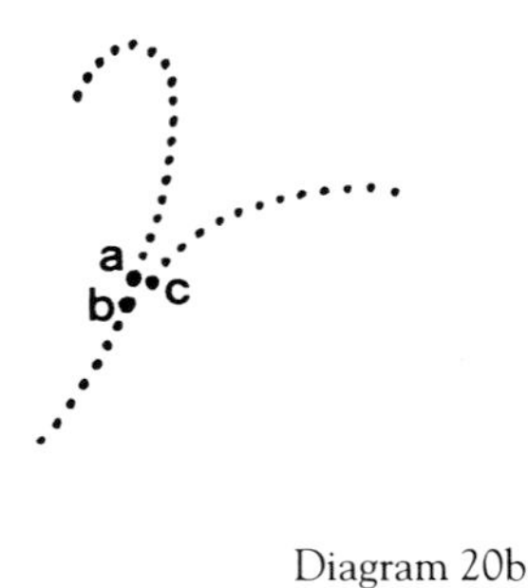

Diagram 20b

Note 20

To get rid of an edge pair when the work meets an already completed braid, as in the side leaves, work down as far as [c], which is the last pinhole before the join. Make up the pinhole here, but do not twist the outer runners, which are sewn into [a] and left to be tied and cut off. Twist the other pair of runners three times and continue working with this pair. Make ordinary pinholes on the outside edge and, when returning to [b], work through the coarse pair (which now lies beside the already completed braid) and, without twisting, attach the runner pair to pinhole [b]. Replace the pin, taking care not to take the threads behind the pin as this creates a loop and, without twisting the sewn-in pair, work back through the coarse pair to the other side.

21 Bird and Chicks

Pricking 21

This pattern is included, even though it has not been worked. Work the front wing first. The head and neck are sewn out into the wing.

The grapes could be worked in the same way as the grapes in Pattern 20.

Note 21

A good pricking is essential to good work. If the holes are out of line or too far apart, alter them as they come to be worked. When pricking from a photocopy, rub over the paper with candle wax, as this lubricates the pricker. If pricking from a poor rubbing, redraw the pattern before pricking it out.

Peacock, detail

22 Peacock

INTERPRETED BY SYLVIA SCARLETT AND CAROLINE BIGGINS

Worked in 120 Thread

Peacock

Working Notes

The peacock was made by two workers. The body and the tail were made separately and then joined by the branch and the leg.

The working order given differs from the photographed work in order to avoid the awkward join between the body and the tail.

Position the pricking so that the body is on the top of the pillow. The pricking can then be moved up to work the lower feathers.

When working the feathers and dividing at [e] to work down either side of the eye, it is more convenient to work both sides simultaneously, as the pins get in the way if one side is too far ahead of the other.

The dainty effect of the rib stitch used for the crown is achieved by working the rib with four pairs. * Cross two pairs through two pairs in whole stitch, put in pin, work two half stitches with each of the two side pairs. Repeat from * for each pinhole.

Diagram 22a

Diagram 22b

Diagram 22

Working Order

1 Work the flower in half stitch with a leadwork centre.

2 Begin leaf stem at [a]. Work up into and around the top divided leaf. Complete the leaf spray.

3 Begin curl with a rib, add a coarse pair as the curl opens out into a braid. Half stitch vein.

4 Work this as 3, crossing leaf stem as work progresses.

5 Work feather [5] (*see* Diagram 22a).

Set up at [b] in a straight line to [c]. Work round the eye and sew out into the start. Save two pairs at [c] and keep threads at [b] long.

Set up again at [d] and work down as far as [e], where the pairs are divided to work down either side of the eye. Three or four of the centre pairs are sewn into the top of the eye and hung back to use for the filling later. Hang in pairs along the bottom of the eye and work each side down to the bottom separately.

Carry these pairs on into [6].

6 At the end of feather [5], cross the coarse, or make a row of pinholes or windows at the join of the tail with the body and continue up the back of the bird as far as [f]. Cut out coarse pair, reduce to a rib and rib down the breast, sewing out into feather [5] at [g].

7 Set up for head at beak tip. Work a snatch hole with a leadwork for the eye. End the face section with a tie back tassel.

8 Work the top of the head from [h] and sew out along the back.

9 & 10 Rib along the top and across the middle of the wing.

11 Work the wing feathers flat or raised, catching the leading runner when crossing the middle rib.

12 Fill in the top of the wing from [j] to [k].

13 Crown. Sew four pairs into the head at [m]. Work up the stem and around the crown (*see* Diagram 22b) and back to the stem. Work the other stems from the crown, sewing out into the head.

14 Feathers [14]–[21]. After completing each feather, add the side feathers.

Fillings

The filling in the feathers is Snowflake.

Peacock, detail

Pricking 22

Note 22

When adding or taking out a pair on a back stitch, take out the pair the first time the pinhole is used. When adding a pair, do this when making up the pinhole.

23 Perched Bird

INTERPRETED BY SUSAN HANNAFORD HILL

Worked in 180 Thread

Perched Bird

Diagram 23

Working Notes

The wings have alternating feathers of Chudleigh Twist (*see* Note 23) and two central half stitches, to give variety.

Use raised sewings when sewing out the many pairs used to work the head, as then the knots lie behind the work and leave a neat row of pinholes where the head joins the wing.

The tail feathers are each ribbed around, but they could be started at the bottom and worked flat. When working a rib on the inside of a curve, use back stitches to get the rib to lie flat.

Pricking 23

Working Order

1 Begin wing at [a], work down to [b], cut out coarse pairs and carry the rib into the lower body.

2 Rib lower body with pairs from [b], turn at [c] and fill in.

3 Sew in rib pairs for the head at [b], hang in pairs for filling in all round the front of the head. Fill in the head, making a small hole for the eye.

4 Beak.

5 Front Wing. Inner row of feathers. Rib and work each feather from [d].

6 Middle row of feathers. Sew in pairs for rib at [e].

7 Outer row of feathers. Sew in pairs for rib at [f].

8 Sew in pairs to rib the body at [g], raise and roll these four feathers and attach them to the lower body.

9 Back Wing. Sew in pairs for rib at [h].

10 Sew in pairs to rib the tail at [j], rib round, hanging in pairs round the bottom to fill in. A coarse pair is added where the braids divide. Carry pairs on for feathers [11], [12] and [13].

14 Sew in pairs for feather [14].

15 Sew in pairs for feather [15].

16 The pairs from feather [16] can be carried on into [17] and [18].

19, 20 & 21 Work each feather separately.

22 Flower. Begin with the inner circle. After joining, carry pairs into scalloped petals.

23 Flower. Rib round the centre and carry rib pairs round each petal, hanging in pairs round the top of each petal for filling in.

24 Leaves.

25 Hoop. Sew the pairs into the leaf and work them round to sew out into the tail.

Fillings

A Four Pin.
B Swing and Pin.
C No Pin.

Note 23

Chudleigh Twist. Sort out three middle pairs. Identify the two downright bobbins on either side of these three pairs with a piece of coloured cotton, as these two pairs remain constant either side of the vein.

Work runners through to the middle three pairs. Twist the runners once and leave them hanging. Twist the last pair they passed through once. Leave.

With the first two of the three middle pairs, make a whole stitch and twist them both once. Leave.

Pick up the last of the three middle pairs and use it to work to the end of the row, twisting the first pair the runners pass through once.

There are now still three pairs in the middle, but they have changed order. By continuously noting the downright pair on either side of the vein it is easy to see which three pairs form the vein.

In the return row the runners are carried right across the row. Work the runners through to the three central downrights. Twist the runners and the last pair they passed through once. Make a whole stitch and one twist with the next three pairs, i.e., the downrights and the runners. Work to the end of the row, twisting the first downright pair the runners pass through once.

Repeat these two rows.

24 Ribbon Handkerchief Corner

INTERPRETED BY SUSAN HANNAFORD HILL

Worked in 180 Thread

Working Notes

The Handkerchief Corner is an adaptation of the wedding veil motif (*see* Pattern 30). It has been done without purls. If a purl edge is used, it would be easier to work it flat, i.e. without the raised edge. It is possible to sew into a purl rib, but remember to leave in the pin whilst taking the sewing, otherwise the purls will pull out (*see* Note 29).

Ribbon Handkerchief Corner

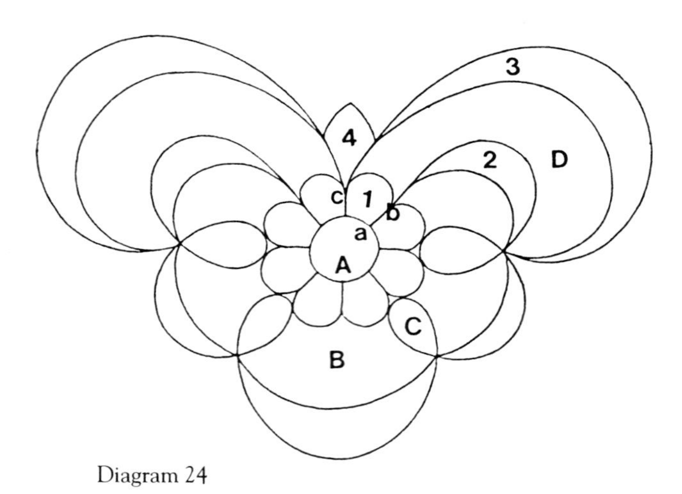

Diagram 24

Pricking 24

Working Order

1 Rib round the centre of the flower from [a] and carry pairs into petal, starting petal on a straight line. When sewing out the flower, keep some of the edge pairs at [b] to carry on into the rib.

2 Hang rib pairs into the flower at [b] and rib round the edge of the ribbon. Work back over, filling in the braids.

3 Sew the rib for the outer ribbon into the top of the flower at [c]. Add a coarse pair for the braid and sew out into ribbon 2.

4 Rib. Hang in pairs for filling in.

Fillings

A No Pin.
B Traffic Lights (Toad in the Hole Variation).
C Whole Stitch Block Variation.
D Leadwork and Lattice.

Note 24

Always anticipate knots and get rid of them while there are at least two inches of thread to spare.

In whole stitch, the bobbin with the knot can be looped around a pin above the work and replaced in the correct position. Cut off the loop with the knot when the section being worked is complete.

Knots in runners and half stitch have to be swapped with one of the bobbins that lie inside the coarse thread, i.e. when the thread with the knot is about to be used as a runner. Make sure it is not the leading bobbin of the runner pair. If it is, give the runner pair an extra twist. After the first whole stitch has been made with the runners and the coarse pair, exchange the downright bobbin inside the coarse thread with the bobbin with the knot. Work on for several rows, then take out in the usual way or hang up the bobbin with a knot on a pin and replace it in the correct position.

It is unnecessary to wind the knots a long way back if only a small piece of work is being made.

25 Ribbon Edging

Worked in 180 Thread

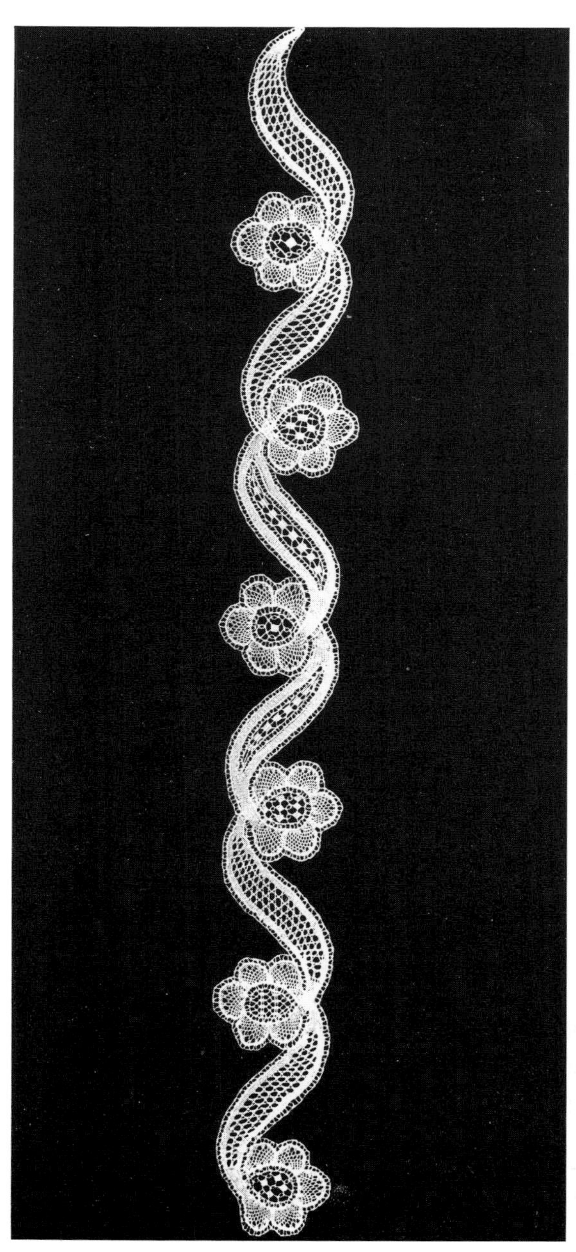

Ribbon Edging

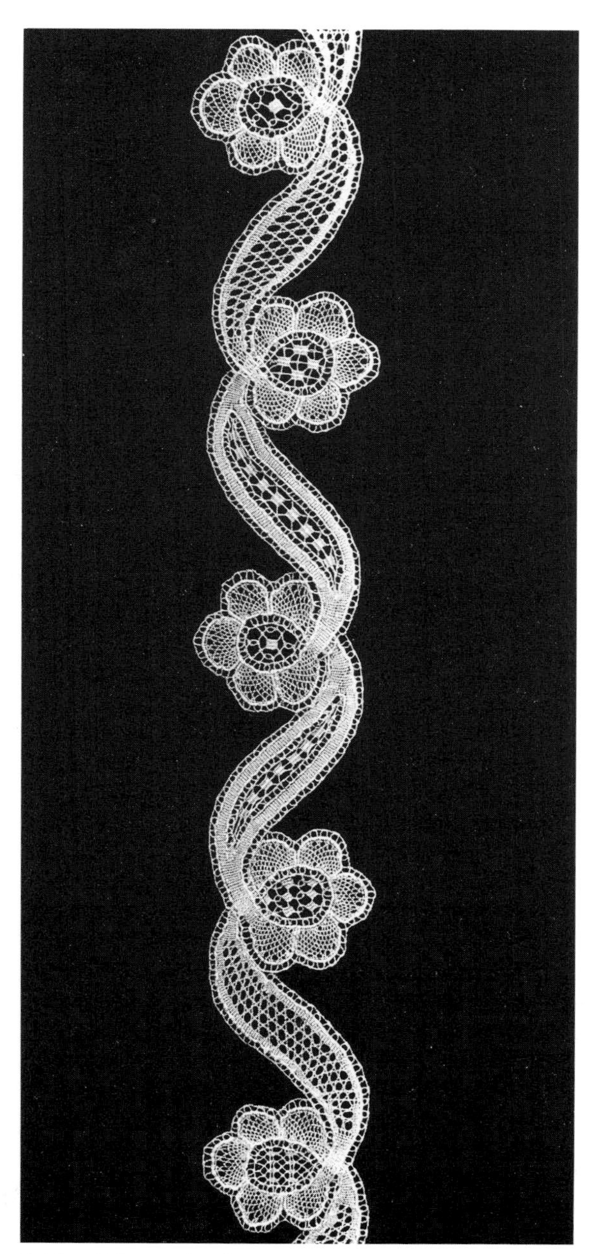

Ribbon Edging, detail

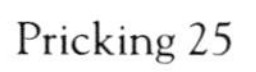

Pricking 25

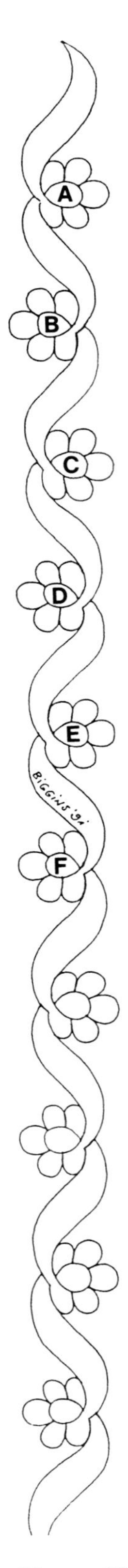

Diagram 25

Working Notes

This simple edging is continuous and includes two different corners. The knot on the coarse bobbin should be wound back a long way, but the knots on the other bobbins only need to go back two or three inches, as they are constantly being taken out and hung in again.

The braids are worked with a double Chudleigh Twist and a divided braid with a leadwork filling. Eighteen pairs are used for both braids. The leadwork filling is worked with three pairs. One pair is sewn into each side of the space to work the leadwork, and one pair is sewn in at the top above the first leadwork. This pair is kept twisted and used with the central leadwork bobbin as a single bobbin, i.e. treat the three bobbins as one.

The flower centres, A, C, D and F, are variations of Swing and Pin. B is Strawberry Variation and E is Italian.

Note 25

Crossing two braids. On approaching the braid to be crossed, make up the last pinhole and work one more row. Sew in all the runner pairs and work two or three rows across the braid, without pins, i.e. as in rib, work through all the bobbins, twist the runner pair once and work back with the last pair they passed through. On reaching the other side of the completed braid, sew in all the runner pairs and continue.

26 Rings and Roundels

Worked in Old 200 Thread

Rings and Roundels, detail (See also p. 12)

Rings and Roundels, detail

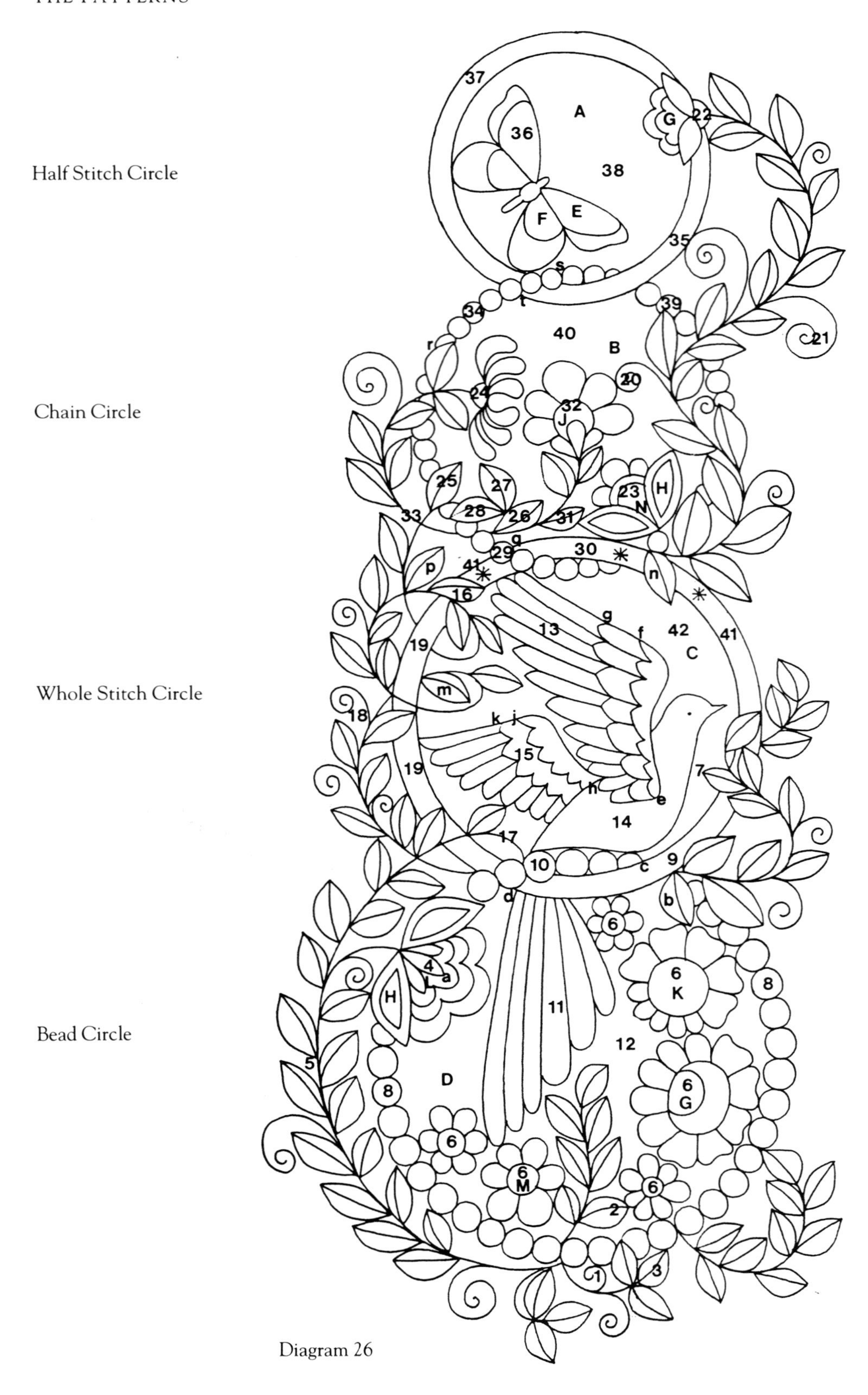
Half Stitch Circle
Chain Circle
Whole Stitch Circle
Bead Circle

Diagram 26

Working Notes

Work this piece on two pillows. The bottom bead circle, the bird, leaves, flowers and all parts of the whole stitch circle (with the exception of the three starred sections of the hoop and the net filling) are worked on one pillow. Leave this work on the pillow. The whole of the top two circles are worked on the second pillow.

When both pieces of work (except for the two remaining starred sections of the hoop and the net filling) are complete, lift the top circles and pin onto the whole stitch circle. Replace pins and pin down about an inch of the chain circle, which is to be joined.

This design has many ribs and tendrils. As a general rule, six pairs are used for the main leaf-bearing ribs and five pairs for the tendrils and raised work.

There are very many small and interlocking leaves, tendrils and circles, so it is often necessary to use two sets of bobbins at once.

There are over a hundred leaves, so use as many different variations as possible for veins, four-pin buds and raised work to avoid boredom!

Working Order

Bottom Two Circles

Bead Circle and Whole Stitch Circle

1 Begin with the tendril and rib into the tip of leaf [2], turn and work back over.

2 Finish this spray of leaves.

3 Sew pairs into first rib and complete spray of three leaves.

4 Start flower at a point [a], work into rib, rib stem and sew into first tendril. Complete flower.

5 Work leaves on stem [4].

6 Work the six flowers in the bottom circle.

7 Start at the tip of this leaf, work, rib down to leaf [b] and sew out into flower. Finish spray.

8 Once these leaves have been worked, complete most of the bottom circle.

9 Work the interlocking of the two bottom circles with two sets of bobbins simultaneously. Work the whole stitch circle down from leaf [7], working well past [c].

10 Sew in the bead circle at [c] and work down to flower [4], sew out. Sew out the whole stitch circle into the bead circle at [d].

11 Work the tail. Begin by ribbing down from [d]. Alternate veins of half stitch and Chudleigh Twist.

12 Work the filling in the bead circle.

13 Upper Wing. Begin scalloped feathers at [e] and work scallops up to [f], crossing the coarse for each feather. At [f], rib into middle row of feathers as far as [g]. Rib and roll down to [e]. Sew in rib at [g] for outer row of feathers.

14 Begin body at beak. Make a small hole for eye. Sew out into bead circle.

15 Lower Wing. Begin scalloped feathers at [h] and work up to [j], crossing the coarse for each feather. Turn at [j] and work a row of scallops down to the body. Sew out. Sew in rib pairs at [k] for outer feathers.

16 Work leaf [16] beginning at leaf tip. Rib round the tip of leaf [m], working back over leaf. Finish spray, except for leaf [p].

17 Rib from bead circle and sew into rib [4]. Finish spray.

18 Sew into rib [16] and sew out into bead circle. Finish spray.

19 Complete these two sections of the whole stitch circle.

Pricking 26a

Pricking 26b

Top Two Circles

Chain Circle and Half Stitch Circle

20 Rib from the tip of the tendril, round into the tip of leaf [n], work back over the leaf and carry pairs into the single link of chain.

21 Rib and Spray. Sew out into rib [20].

22 Start calyx of flower on a straight line, rib down into rib [21]. Finish flower.

23 Flower.

24 Start honeysuckle by ribbing round the calyx. Turn and fill. Rib up into the petals.

25 Work leaf. Rib round stem and up to the tip of leaf [p]. Turn and fill in.

26 Work leaf. Leave pairs hanging.

27 Work leaf. Sew into leaf [26].

28 Work leaf. Sew into leaf [26]. Work tiny piece of chain by sewing rib into leaf [25]. Work on into leaf [28]. Sew out into leaf [27].

29 Work chain circle down from leaf [28]. Leave pairs hanging when they are well past [q]. Sew out pairs hanging from leaf [26].

30 Sew in pairs for whole stitch circle at [q]. Sew out whole stitch circle into leaf [n]. Sew chain circle into whole stitch circle.

31 Work leaf and sew out into leaf [26].

32 Sew rib for flower into leaf [31] and rib up into calyx. Work flower.

33 Sew rib for honeysuckle stem into chain circle and sew out into honeysuckle. Complete spray.

34 Sew in rib for chain circle at [r]. Rib both sides as far as [s]. Leave pairs hanging.

35 Sew pairs into chain circle at [t] for half stitch circle. Work round and out into flower [22]. Sew out chain circle into half stitch circle.

36 Butterfly Body and Wings.

37 Complete half stitch circle.

38 When the half stitch circle is complete, the filling can be worked.

39 Complete all the small links in the chain circle.

40 Work the chain circle filling.
Lift the two complete top circles and pin onto the whole stitch circle.

41 Work the two remaining starred sections of the whole stitch circle.

42 Fill in the background of the whole stitch circle.

Fillings

A Blossom.
B Blow Brain.
C Net.
D Four Pin.
E Whole Stitch Block Variation.
F Toad in the Hole with Enclosed Pinholes.
G Swing and Pin.
H Italian.
J Pin and Stitch.
K Toad in the Hole Variation.
L Devon Cutworks.
M No Pin.
N Swing and Stitch.

Note 26

Raised sewings are always preferable when finishing work, as then the knots and bunches lie slightly behind the work and are not visible from the right side.

27 Rocking Horse

INTERPRETED BY ELIZABETH FOLLAND

Worked in 120 Thread

Rocking Horse, wrong side

Working Notes

As with many of the patterns in this book, the Rocking Horse is a good subject for individual interpretation. There is a photograph of the wrong side of the work, as much of the detail is backed with half stitch.

Start the chain rib down the neck of the horse at the top in a straight line, divide the pairs in half, work both sides down to the first join, and cross the ribs by working the two sets through each other.

Two whole stitches are used as a division in the half stitch legs and as decoration in the tail.

If the rib pinholes are on the inside of the curve, remember to backstitch to get the rib to lie flat.

Rocking Horse, right side

Working Order

1 Work harness from [a], ending with a tie back tassel at [b]. (An alternative way of starting is to set up rib pairs at [j], rib round the circle, join at [j] and work back over, saving pairs at [k] for the rib down to [m]. Work the small piece of harness from [b] and sew it to the completed circle.)

2 Start braid at [c] and work across in whole stitch, reducing to a rib under the cheek and sewing out at [d].

3 Work the decorative chain down the neck, beginning on a straight line with the three holes at [e] and crossing the ribs through each other. For the final crossing at [f], lie the two sets of rib one over the other.

4 Work one set of the rib pairs down to [g] and leave.

5 Use the other set of rib pairs left at [f] to rib up the horse's neck as far as [h]. Turn the pairs here and work into the harness, sewing out at [j].

6 Leadworks, or other decoration in neck chain.

7 Rib around ear from [h] to [c].

8 Wind the knots well back. Sew rib pairs into the harness at [k], rib down to [m] laying in pairs at each pinhole. Work back in half stitch over the whole face (working over the harness and catching it in occasionally). Work to within one row of the beginning of the eye.

9 One row before the eye, make a whole stitch with the two pairs above the pinhole that will start the eye.

10 Divide for the eye by working back to the two whole stitch pairs and one more pair. Leave the runners and complete as for snatch pin hole with leadwork. Alternatively, divide the braid into two, work up both sides of the eye and add the leadwork afterwards.

11 Increase pairs to take in the ear whilst backstitching on the neck side.

12 Sew out pairs as the ear is finished.

13 Bring runners out to the outside edge and leave. Top sew the downrights into the top edge of the harness before using them to work down the neck. The bunch of five or six pairs on the inside neck edge at [n] need not be sewn in, but can be brought in gradually as the neck is worked to save constant sewings at [n].

14 Work across neck. The pairs left at [n] can be brought in one at a time, tied and used as runners to save backstitching on this tight bend. Work down as far as [g] catching the chain decoration occasionally with the runners. Sew out at [g], leaving the original six pairs of rib for use later.

15 Sew in rib pairs for the mane at [h] and roll them up the ear and into the mane. Rib and roll the mane down to [p] putting purls on the outside of the mane.

16 Use the mane pairs to rib across the back to [r] hanging in pairs at [q] to work round the saddle. Leave the rib pairs at [r].

17 Pick up the pairs left at [q], add a coarse pair and work round the saddle braid back to [p].

18 Return to the rib pairs left at [r]. Rib and roll around the saddle design, back to [p]. Sew out into rib.

19 Pick up rib pairs left at [g] and rib under belly, picking up ribbed loops. Rib up to [r] hanging in and laying back pairs for filling in.

20 Use these rib pairs and the extra pairs sewn into pinholes between [r–q] to work back over the end of the body and round the saddle, bringing in the laid back pairs round to where the mane joins the body at [p].

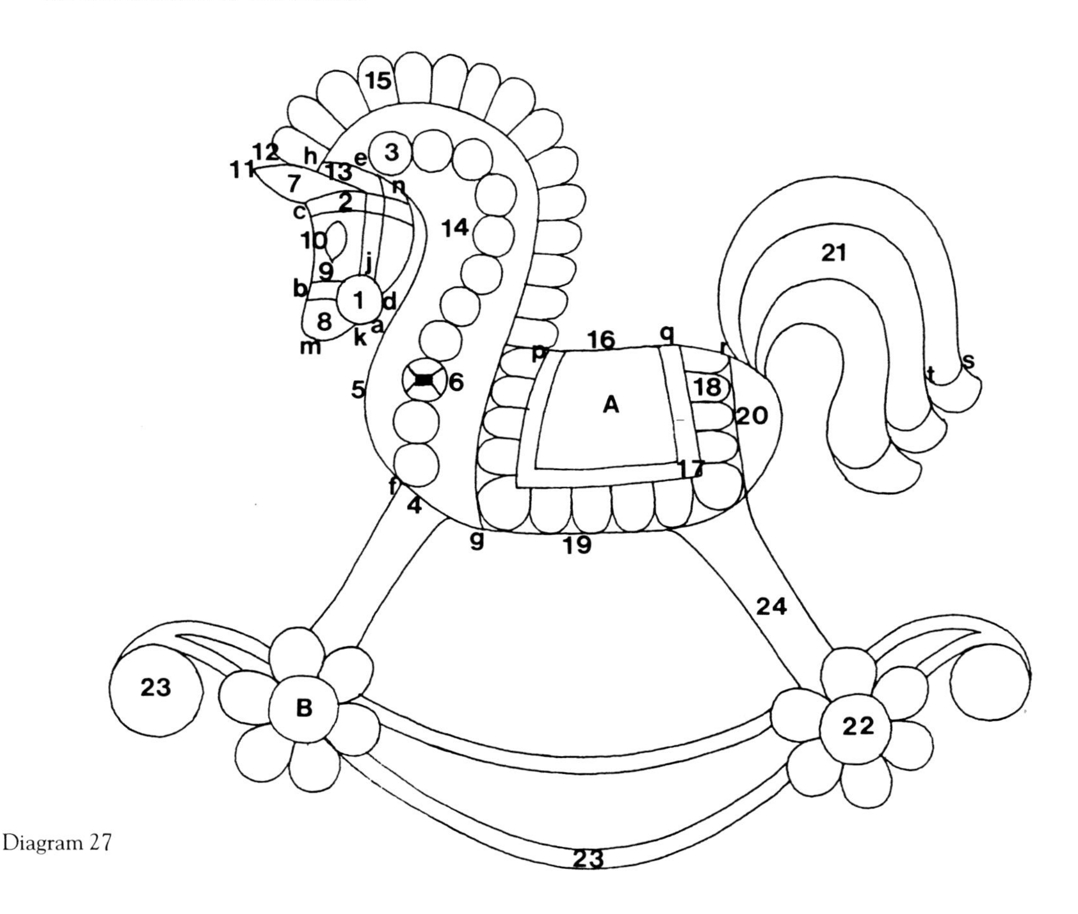

Diagram 27

Pricking 27

21 Tail. Sew in rib pairs near [r]. Rib up to [s]. Leave rib pairs and hang in pairs across the line from [s] to [t] in the same way as when starting on a straight line. Return to the rib pairs at [s]. Continue the rib round to [t] and join the pairs into the braid. Work down to sew into the body and roll pairs up into the next section.

22 Flowers.

23 Rockers.

24 Legs. Sew into the body and out into the flower.

Fillings

A Toad in the Hole with Enclosed Pinholes.
B No Pin.

Note 27

Rib is mainly worked with the pinholes on the outside of the curve. If, however, the rib has to go around the inside of a curve, backstitch in the usual way so that the rib lies flat.

28 Summer Bouquet

Interpreted by Mary de Salis

Worked in Egyptian Cotton 120

Summer Bouquet

Working Notes

The pricking for the Summer Bouquet is 25 per cent smaller than the actual work.

The work is made in two parts and can be joined by the starred central stem. If the work has to be removed from the pillow, pin the pricking, with the lace attached, onto a polystyrene tile so that it keeps its shape while the other parts are being worked. The many leaves have a great variety of different veins, spots and buds.

Summer Bouquet, detail

Working Order

Section One

1 Rib round the centre of the ribbon from [a], join the rib and carry the rib pairs on into the leaf spray. Complete this spray and the leaves on the other side.

2 Start the ribbon on a straight line from [b]. Sew the ribbon out into the central ring. Complete the ribbons, beginning at the tips and sewing out into the completed braids.

3 The decorative ring is worked round, disregarding the stems. Beginning at [c], work the top circle and join. Save four pairs to work the purl pin bars. Work over the top in whole stitch.

4 Work ribs round the centre, and petals of the flower from [d] and [e]. The rib round the petals will need back stitches in the indents to help the rib to stay flat. Join the inner rib ring and work out on a straight line to meet the petal rib. Work back over in half stitch. Make two rows of whole stitch between the petals.

5 Rib round the centre of the flower from [f] and carry the rib pairs on into the whole stitch petal. Turn and fill in. Sew rib pairs into the central ring on the other side at [g] for the other large whole stitch petal. The rest of the petals are worked flat.

6 Rib the central ring. Join the rib and carry the pairs on round the petals. Fill the petals with half stitch.

7 The small half stitch flowers have a rib centre.

8 Sew rib pairs into flower [7]. Rib up the stem and up the side of the bud, work back over and carry pairs on to rib up the other side of the bud. Turn and work back over. Set up purl rib pairs at [h] and work round to the bud, add two pairs into the rib to work over the top of the bud. Cut out the two pairs and continue the purl rib to end with a tie back tassel at [j].

Finish all the stems and leaves on this half of the pattern. When working the stems down from the flowers to the decorative ring, remove the pins from the top of the ring and fold it back until all the stems are worked and sewn out. Let the ring come back into place and re-pin.

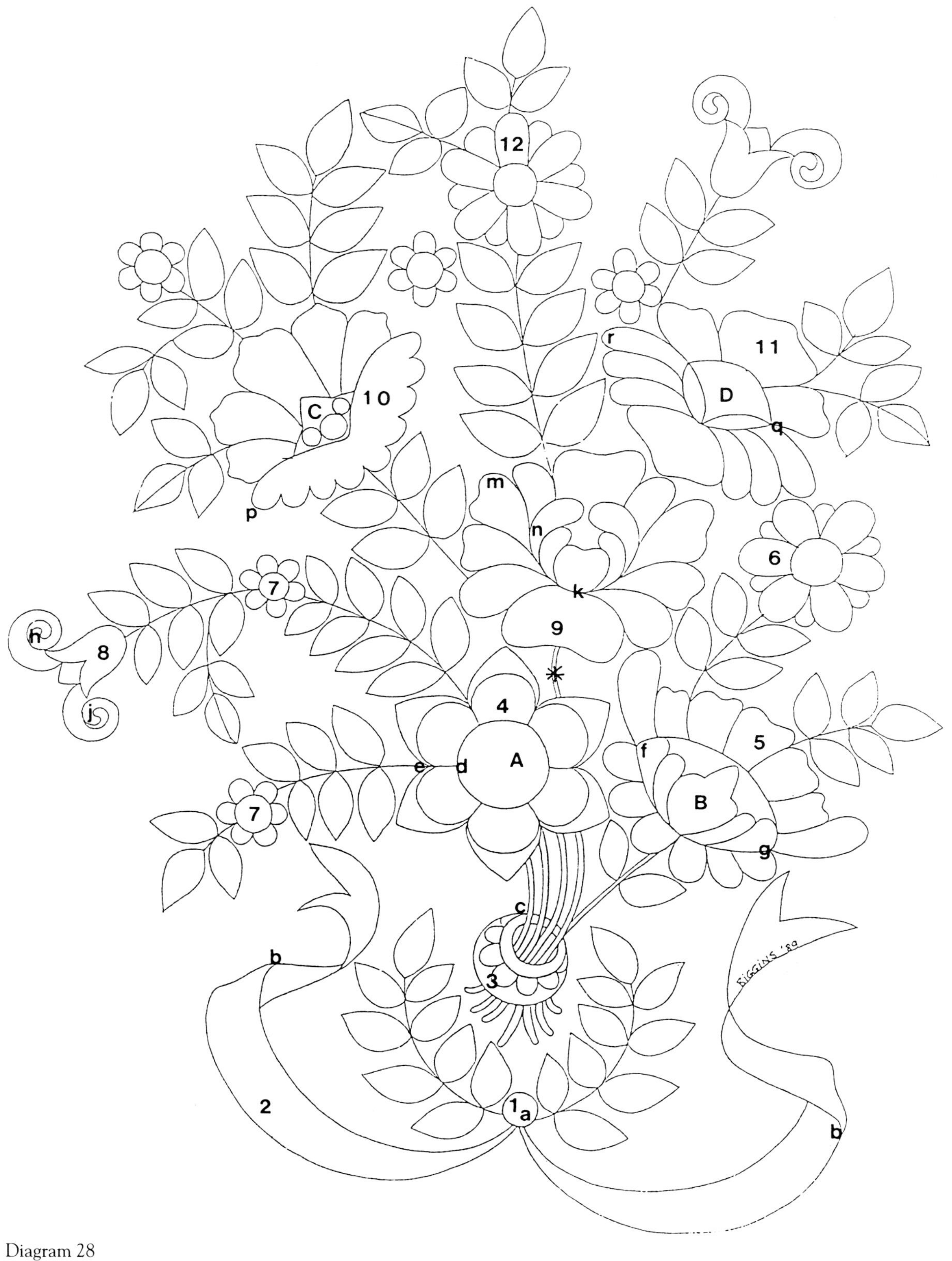

Diagram 28

Pricking 28

Section Two

9 Set up rib pairs at [k]. Work round the bottom petal, join the rib and carry these rib pairs up to the top of the petal [m], turn and work these three side petals. Repeat for the other side. Sew in rib pairs for the centre petals at [n]. Fill the top and bottom petals in from side to side.

The leaves on the stem above flower [9] have single and double Chudleigh Twists (*see* Note 23).

10 Set up rib pairs at [p], rib the top of the petal and work back over in half stitch, with a purl edge. Rib round the centre of the flower. Rib round the top petals. The leaves of the central leaf spray above the flower are decorated with raised leadwork spots (*see* Note 28).

11 Set up rib pairs at [q], rib round the centre, join the rib and fill in the two inner whole stitch petals. Carry the rib pairs on into the top of the side petal [r]. Work these three side petals. Repeat for the other side. Rib and fill remaining petals.

12 Rib round the central ring. The petals are worked flat. The half stitch petals have two whole stitches at each edge.

Fillings

A Leadwork and Lattice.
B Double Blossom with Leadworks.
C Toad in the Hole Variation.
D Four Pin with Leadworks.

Note 28

Raised leadwork spots. Work down to where the spot is to be made. Decide on the width of the leadwork and select the two downright pairs either side of this width. Twist these pairs once before and after the leadwork in whole stitch – twice if the spots are made in half stitch. The leadwork can be made first, leaving the runners at the edge, and then backed with whole or half stitch. Alternatively, leaving the two selected pairs hanging, work three or four rows of the backing over these two pairs and then work the leadwork with the two hanging pairs – it will automatically slide up under the completed work. Replace the leadwork pairs in the correct position at the bottom and continue working.

29 Wedding Veil Spray

Interpreted by Alison Gibbs

Worked in 180 Thread

Wedding Veil Spray

Working Notes

This design was inspired by lace on an old wedding veil. The use of so many different veins in the leaves and the variety of buds makes the modern version more lively.

For sewing into a pearl rib *see* Note 29.

Wedding Veil Spray, old lace

Pricking 29

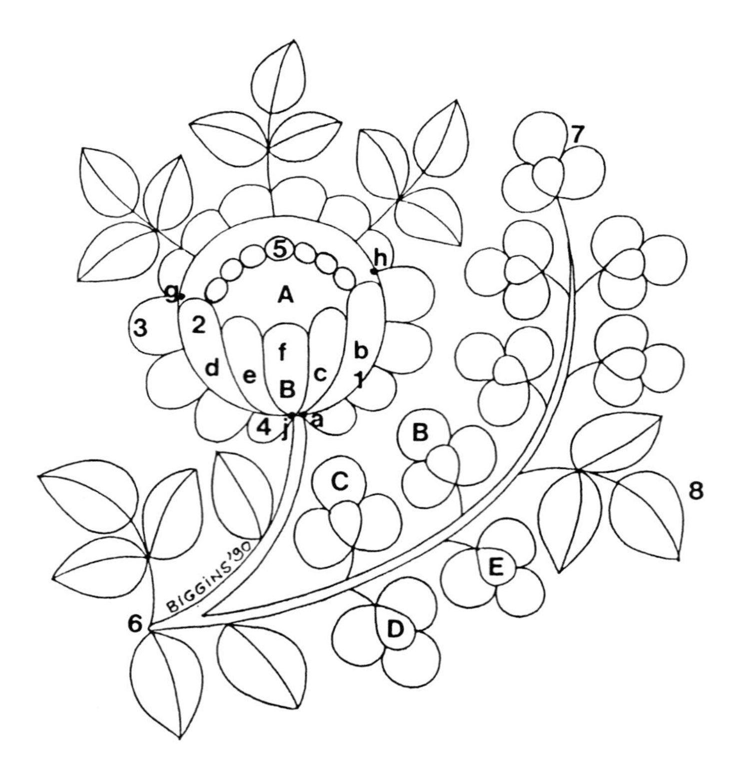

Diagram 29

Working Order

1 Flower. Set up rib pairs at [a] and work in an anti-clockwise direction round the inner edge of the flower. Join the rib at [a] and carry the rib pairs up the edge of petal [b]. Hang in pairs across the top, turn and work back over. Sew out into the rib. Some of these pairs may be carried in rib up the edge of petal [c]. Add in pairs across the top. Turn and work back over, sewing out into the rib. Make a tie back tassel and leave ends long.

2 Sew rib pairs into the central ring for petal [d] and work rib up to turn at the top. Work petal [e] the same. For petal [f], rib across the top of the petal, laying extra pairs to the back at each hole. Sew in pairs to work Devon Cutwork, then use laid back pairs to back with half stitch.

3 Sew in pairs for the pearl rib at [g] and work the petal outlines down to [j]. Keep these pairs for filling in later. Do the same for the other side, sewing in rib pairs at [h]. These can be cut out at [a].

4 Fill the petals with half stitch, starting in a clockwise direction from [j] and working round to [a]. An edge pair will need to be added for the top flat petals.

5 Work the chain in the flower centre by sewing two sets of five pairs into petal [d] on the left side. Work in rib with the pinholes on the outside, to the first crossover. Work the runners to the inner edge on both braids. Take the inner pair from the left braid through the four downrights of the right braid. Work the remaining left braid downright pairs through the right braid downright pairs. Pull up tightly. The middle two pairs now become runners, which continue in rib. Repeat crossover process and sew out into petal [b] on the right hand side.

6 Start the stem at the bottom and divide for the two branches. Work the braid up to sew

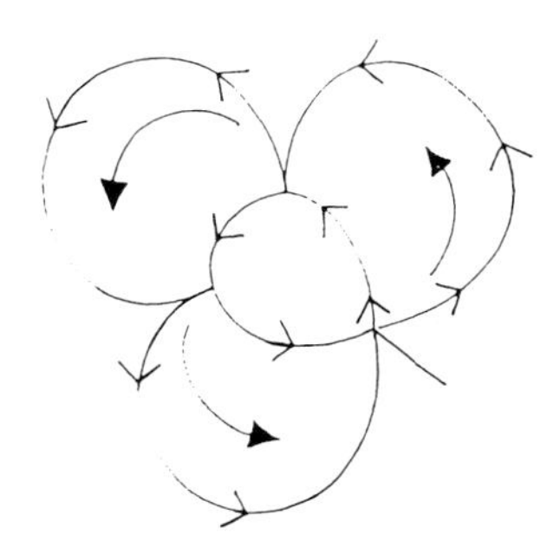

Diagram 29a

out into the flower. Cut out the coarse pair when the rib of the bud branch is reached and carry the rib pairs into the trefoil.

7 The trefoils all have a ribbed outline. The centre petal of the top trefoil is worked from the top to the centre, where the pairs are sewn into the central ring. All these pairs are used either to work the centre or to carry on into the left and right hand petals. All the other trefoils are outlined in rib and have a variety of fillings. Carry the rib pairs over to fill in the whole and half stitch petals.

8 The leaves are all variations of divided leaves with Chudleigh Twist, ladder trail and whole and half stitch veins. Rib the raised leaves up the centre and work down over the rib. Roll up the other side and work back over.

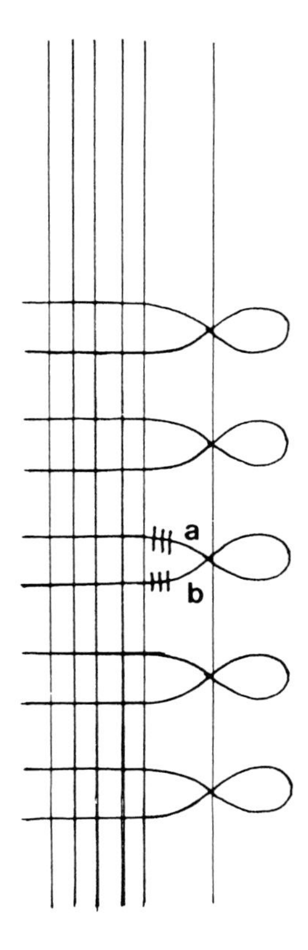

Diagram 29b

Fillings

A Four Pin Flower with Leadwork.
B Devon Cutwork.
C Pin and Stitch with Leadwork.
D Snowflake.
E Blossom.

Note 29

Sewing into a purl rib. Refer to Diagram 29b. A raised sewing can be taken into the top or bottom bar [a] or [b], but remember to leave the pin in the purl, as if it is removed the purl will pull out.

30 Wedding Veil Edging

Worked in 180 Thread

Wedding Veil Edging

Working Notes

The inspiration for this wedding veil edging came from the old lace shown in the photograph.

Work the flower and leaves motifs first, then join the braid with the scroll motif. Work two flower motifs and pin them back onto the pillow at either end of the joining braid.

The two motifs shown are worked very differently. The pattern with the raised edge round the ribbon braid and raised buds takes much longer to complete than the flat motif.

Working Order

Flower and Leaves Motif

1 Refer to Diagram 30. Begin flower at [a], starting on a straight line.

2 Work the loop from [b] to [c], cutting out the coarse threads where the braid narrows to a rib and ending with a tie back tassel.

3 Hang in rib pairs at [d] for a raised edge to the ribbons, or hang in pairs plus a coarse pair at [e] for flat work. If a coarse pair is used, leave it behind at [f] where the rib loop works down to join the flower, and pick it up again for the next section of braid. Work round to [g]. If working a rib edge the pairs will need to be rolled for the last few pinholes before [g], where the work is turned to work back over. Add a coarse bobbin and one other on the inner edge, before commencing the braid.

Wedding Veil Edging, detail

Diagram 30

4 The leaves and buds may be worked in a variety of ways, starting at [h] at either the tip of the leaf or top of the vein. Work down into the stem and sew out into the ribbon.

5 Sew six pairs into the loop at [j]. Add a coarse pair where the rib widens into a braid. Begin the purls when just past the joining section at [k]. Add in pairs. Nineteen pairs were used for the photographed work. Sew into the loop at the other side at [m]. Work another flower motif and join the two with the scroll and braid sections. Pin one on to each end of Pricking 30b.

Scroll and Braid

6 Set up four pairs and a coarse pair at [n]. Work down to [p] adding pairs so that there are sixteen pairs at [p] to make the work dense enough to divide the braid into two.

7 Work up to nineteen pairs in each braid and attach them to the flower motif at [q].

8 Begin scrolls at [r] and sew them out at [n].

9 Sew in rib pairs for the petals at [s], rib round the bottom of the petals. Outline each petal, hanging in pairs round the top and completing each petal before commencing the next. Save some of the pairs from the petals for the filling.

Fillings

A Jubilee.
B Four Pin.
C Blossom.
D Swing and Pin.
E Snowflake.
F Six Pin, Toad in the Hole.
G Italian.
H Traffic Lights (Toad in the Hole Variation).
J Devon Cutworks.
K No Pin.
L Daisy.

Wedding Veil Edging, old lace

Prickings 30a and 30b

Note 30

When attaching a lace edging to a wedding veil, the edge of the net is first stitched onto wide strips of sugar paper to support it whilst attaching the lace. Stitch the lace onto the net in small sections. First tack it in place on the net. Oversew the lace to the net with the thread used to make the lace, sewing into each hole of the inner edge. Cut the surplus net away after the border has been attached and the paper removed.

If long lengths are to be joined on the pillow, roll the unsupported work round a small cardboard tube between a layer of tissue paper, which can be pinned to the pillow in the most convenient position.

Store the lace in acid-free tissue paper, away from the light.

FILLINGS

Devon County Show 1990, Second, Alison Gibbs

1 Blow Brain

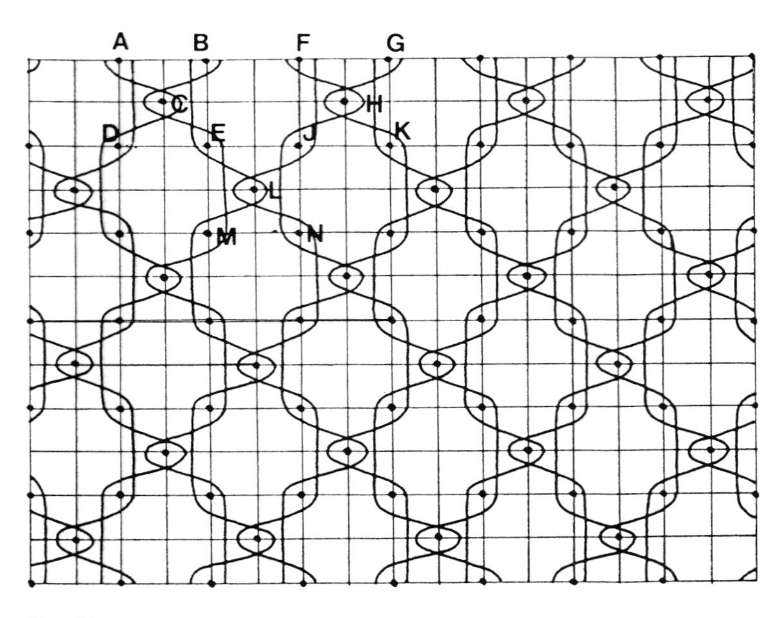

Blow Brain

Blow Brain is not purely a Honiton filling, although it was adapted from a Honiton trolley edging. It can be found in variations in other laces.

It is worked in groups of five holes, the two bottom holes of one group being the two top holes of the next group.

1 Sew in two pairs above each pinhole. With each two pairs, make a whole stitch and three twists, pin, whole stitch and three twists.

2 Make a whole stitch, three twists with the right hand pair from (A) and the left hand pair from (B), pin (C), whole stitch, three twists.

3 Make a whole stitch, three twists with the left hand pair from (A) and the left hand pair from (C), pin (D), whole stitch, three twists.

4 Make a whole stitch, three twists with the right hand pair from (B) and the right hand pair from (C), pin (E), whole stitch, three twists.

Work the five holes, (F), (G), (H), (J), and (K), the same way.

In the next row, (E) and (J) are the top two holes of the block of five holes. The right hand pair from (E) and the left hand pair from (J) make pinhole (L). The left hand pair from (E) and the left hand pair from (L) make pinhole (M), and the right hand pair from (J), with the right hand pair from (L), make pinhole (N).

2 Daisy

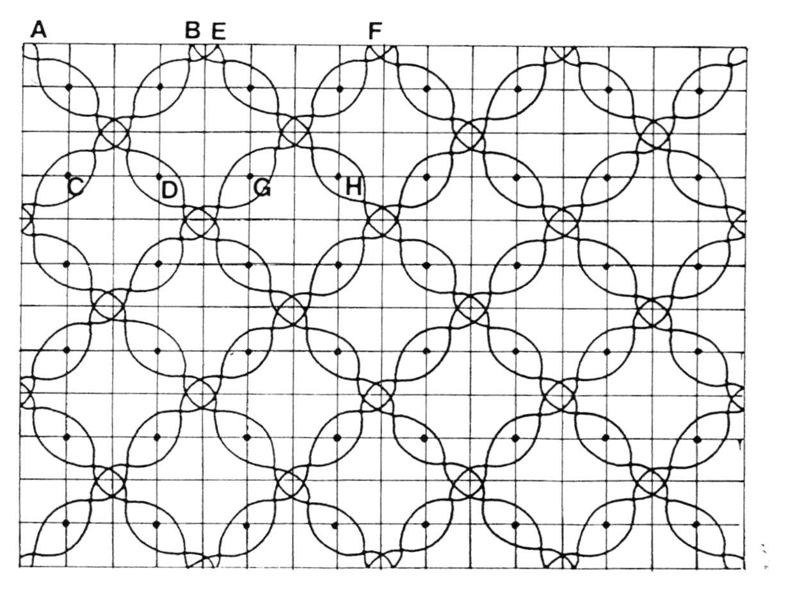

Daisy

Daisy can be pricked on the same grid pricking used for Pin and Chain. For a tiny flower, prick a hole on every intersection of 1 mm graph paper. Work this filling diagonally or horizontally.

1 Sew in two pairs above each pinhole. Make a whole stitch, three twists, pin, whole stitch (no twists) with each two pairs.

2 Weave the two pairs from (A) through the two pairs from (B) in whole stitch. Make a whole stitch and three twists with each two pairs and set pins (C) and (D) between them. Enclose with a whole stitch (no twists).

Work the daisies across the row to the right. In the next row, the daisies come in alternate spaces, i.e. (D) and (G) are the top two holes of the first daisy.

N.B. If the pricking is made on every intersection of 1 mm graph paper, when crossing the four pairs use each pair as one bobbin and make a whole stitch with them. This makes a smaller crossing in the tiny space.

3 Double Blossom with Leadworks

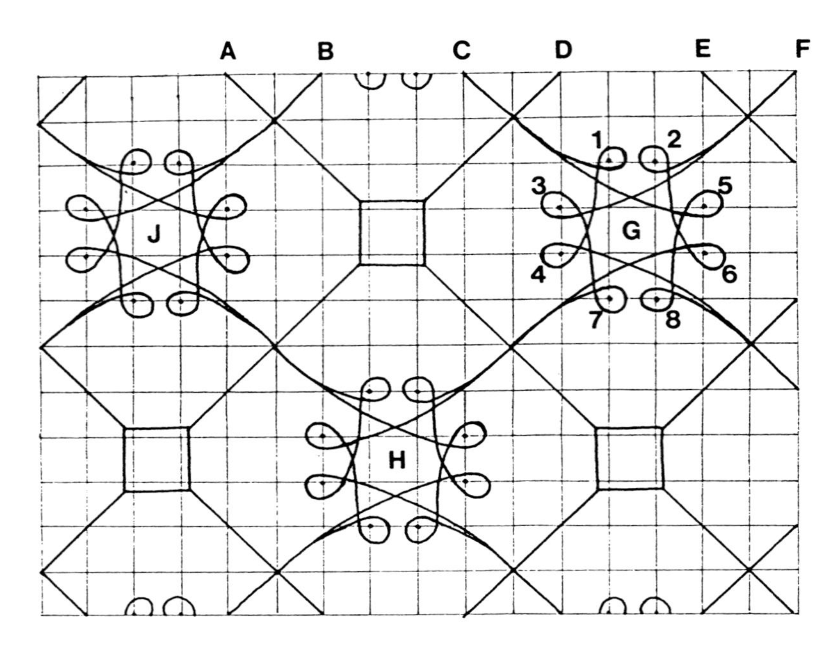

Double Blossom with Leadworks

Use this filling for a large space. The leadwork pairs weave through the pairs that work the blossoms. The leadworks need to be quite substantial.

Sew in two pairs for the plaits at (B), (C) and (F).

Sew in one pair for the leadworks at (A), (D) and (E).

With the two pairs from (C), make a half stitch plait that reaches half way towards the blossom. Do the same with the two pairs from (F) and (B).

Twist the leadwork pairs from (A) and (D) between five and seven times (depending upon the distance from the edge). Weave the pair from (A) through plait (B), and the pair from (D) through plait (C). Twist the leadwork pairs seven times and leave. Continue with the half stitch plaits until they reach the blossom.

Do the same with the pairs from (E) and (F).

Work Blossom (G) with the plaits from (C) and (F).

1 With the right hand pair of the left hand plait, make a right hand purl in hole (1). Whole stitch with the two left hand pairs. Twist both pairs once.

2 With the left hand pair of the right hand plait, make a left hand purl in (2). Whole stitch with the two right hand pairs. Twist both pairs once.

3 Whole stitch with the two centre pairs. Twist both pairs once.

4 Whole stitch with the two left hand pairs, with the left of these two pairs make a left hand purl in (3). Whole stitch, twist both pairs once.

5 With the left hand pair of these two pairs, make a left hand purl in (4). Whole stitch, twist both pairs once.

6 Whole stitch with the two right hand pairs. With the right of these two pairs, make a right hand purl in (5). Whole stitch, twist both pairs once.

7 With the right hand pair of these two pairs, make a right hand purl in (6). Whole stitch, twist both pairs once.

8 Whole stitch with the two centre pairs. Twist both pairs once.

9 Make a whole stitch with the two left hand pairs. With the right hand pair of these two pairs, make a right hand purl in (7). Whole stitch, twist both pairs once.

10 Make a whole stitch with the two right hand pairs. With the left hand pair of these two pairs, make a left hand purl in (8). Whole stitch, twist both pairs once.

This completes blossom (G). The two pairs from hole (7) make a half stitch plait to reach diagonally down to blossom (H), which is worked with the two right hand pairs from blossom (J). The leadwork pairs are twisted seven times and weave through the plaits half way between the blossoms.

4 Leadwork and Pinhole

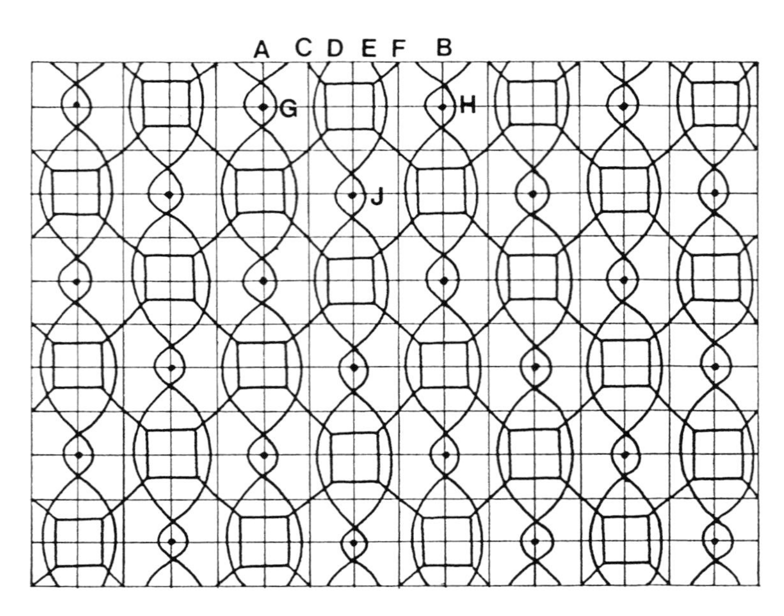

Leadworks with Pinhole

As can be seen from the diagram, the pairs used to make the pinhole circle round the leadwork, and the pairs used for the leadworks pass diagonally to the row below.

The threads around the pins are twisted three times, and the threads that circle the side of the leadworks are twisted three times. At all other times, the pairs are twisted twice.

1 Sew in two pairs above pinholes (A) and (B), and four pairs singly in the pinholes between (A) and (B) from (C) to (F).

2 With the two pairs from (A), make a whole stitch, three twists, pin (G), whole stitch and two twists.

3 Do the same with the two pairs above (B) making pinhole (H).

4 Twist the pairs from (C), (D), (E) and (F) twice. Take (C) through (D) in whole stitch, twist (C) twice and (D) three times.

5 Take (E) through (F) in whole stitch, twist (E) three times and (F) twice.

6 Make a leadwork with the pairs from (C) and (F), twist both pairs twice.

7 With the left hand leadwork pair and the twisted pair from (D), make a whole stitch and twist twice.

8 With the right hand leadwork pair and the twisted pair from (E), make a whole stitch and twist twice.

9 With the pairs from (D) and (E), which have circled round the leadwork, make a whole stitch, twist both pairs three times, and put in pin (J) below leadwork just made. Cover with a whole stitch and two twists.

5 Margaret Maidment's Four Pin Blocks

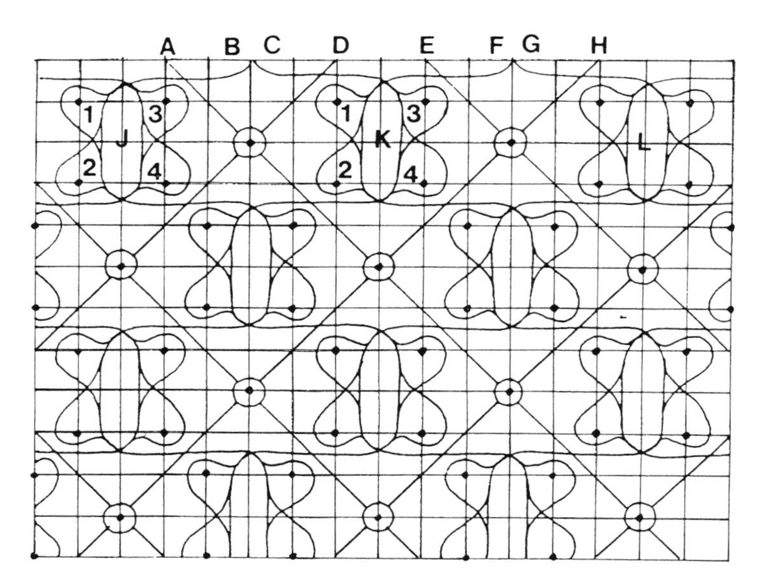

Margaret Maidment's Four Pin Blocks

This filling needs to be pulled up very well and frequently.

1 Sew in one pair for the half stitch pinhole at (A), (D), (E) and (H). Twist these pairs three times. Sew in six pairs for the whole stitch plaits between (B) and (C) and six pairs between (F) and (G).

2 Working with the six pairs between (B) and (C), the three left hand pairs work through the three right hand pairs in whole stitch: the third pair through three pairs to the right, the second pair through three pairs to the right, and the first pair through three pairs to the right. Pull up well, with three pairs on the left and three pairs on the right.

3 With the left hand three pairs, make a whole stitch plait (right hand pair through two pairs to the left). Repeat until the braid is long enough, i.e., half way to block (J).

4 Take the pinhole pair from (A) through this braid and twist it four times. Continue the whole stitch braid until it reaches block (J). Work a similar plait with the three pairs from (C) and also the three pairs from (F), remembering to take the pinhole pair through the braid when it reaches half way.

5 The single pinholes are made with four twists coming down to the pinhole, half stitch, three twists, pin, half stitch and three twists.

6 Make the block of four holes with the right hand plait from between (B) and (C) and the left hand plait from between (F) and (G). Cross the two sets of pairs as in (2) and

pull up well. With the left hand pairs, work the third pair on the right through two pairs to the left, twist three times, put in pin (1). With these runners, work two whole stitches to the right. Repeat for hole (2), i.e., use the same pair as runners.

7 With the right hand pairs, work the first pair on the left through the two pairs on the right, twist three times, put in pin (3). With these runners work two whole stitches to the left. Repeat for hole (4), using the same pair as runners.

8 Cross all six pairs in whole stitch. This completes the Four Pin Block.

6 Snowflake

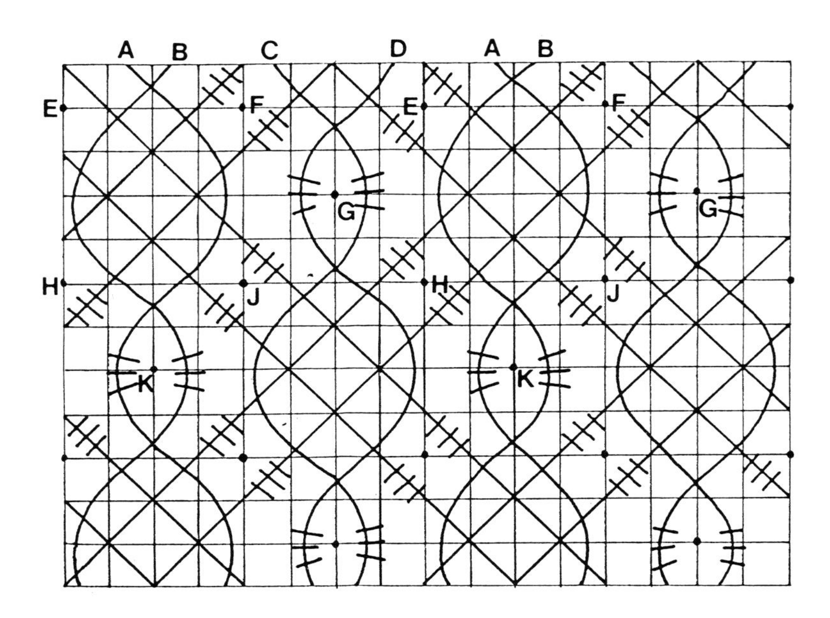

Snowflake

The Snowflake filling can be found in old Honiton lace as well as in other laces. The pricking is the same grid pricking used for Blow Brain.

This is a complicated filling and can be more easily worked from the diagram. Each line represents a pair of bobbins. Lines crossing indicate a whole stitch. The small dashes on the lines show the number of twists.

Work Snowflake diagonally from right to left. Each Snowflake takes six pairs. Check that there are pairs sewn in at (C) and (D) for pinhole (G).

1 Lengthen the pair from (A) and the pair from (B). Make a whole stitch with them.

2 Work the left hand long pair through the two pairs to the left, which come in on either side of pin (E).

3 Work the right hand long pair through the two pairs to the right, which come in on either side of pin (F).

4 Work the two left hand centre pairs through the two right hand centre pairs in whole stitch.

5 Take the outside long pairs to the middle in whole stitch. Make a whole stitch, three twists, pin (K), whole stitch (no twists) with these two pairs.

6 Twist the two side pairs on either side, three times each and put pins (H) and (J) between them in the side holes.

7 Strawberry Variation

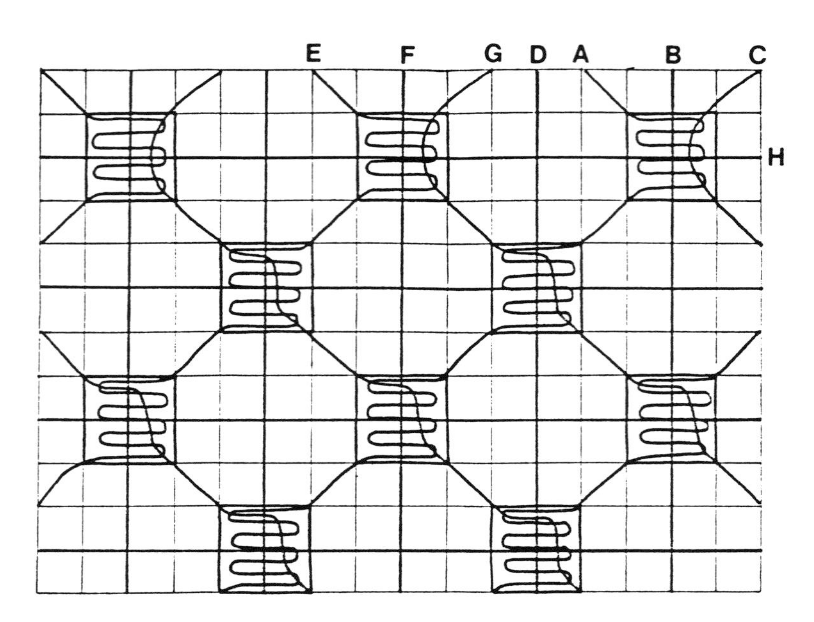

Strawberry Variation

Strawberry is a leadwork filling, with the leadworks worked horizontally, rather than diagonally (as in No Pin). It is worked without a pricking.

The variation has a twisted pair running through the centre of the leadwork, both horizontally and vertically.

1 Sew in two pairs for each leadwork, i.e. one pair from (A) and one from (C). Sew in one pair at (B) to go down vertically through the leadwork, and one pair at (D) to go down past the leadwork. This pair will go down through the leadwork in the next row. Sew in one pair on the right hand side at (H).

2 Work across the row from right to left. For each three leadwork pairs, twist the two outside pairs (E) and (G) three times. Twist the middle pair (F) seven to ten times.

3 Using the second bobbin from the left of these three pairs, make half a leadwork, treating the twisted downright pair from (F) and the inner bobbin from (G) as one bobbin.

4 Twist the pair from (H) three times and work it in whole stitch through the leadwork, still treating the three central downright pairs as one.

5 Twist the pair from (D) three times and make a whole stitch with this pair and the horizontal pair from (H). Twist the horizontal pair three times and the pair from (D) seven times.

6 Repeat to the end of the row, pull up firmly and sew out the horizontal runner pair.

7 Complete the second half of each leadwork.

8 Isolate the pair going down vertically through the leadwork and ensure that only three twists remain on this pair.

9 Twist both leadwork pairs three times.

10 In the next row, work the leadworks diagonally below those worked in the row above. Use the same weaver used in the previous row, i.e. the weaver in the previous row ends second from the left so it will need to work half a row to get it into the second position in the leadwork below.

8 Taunton

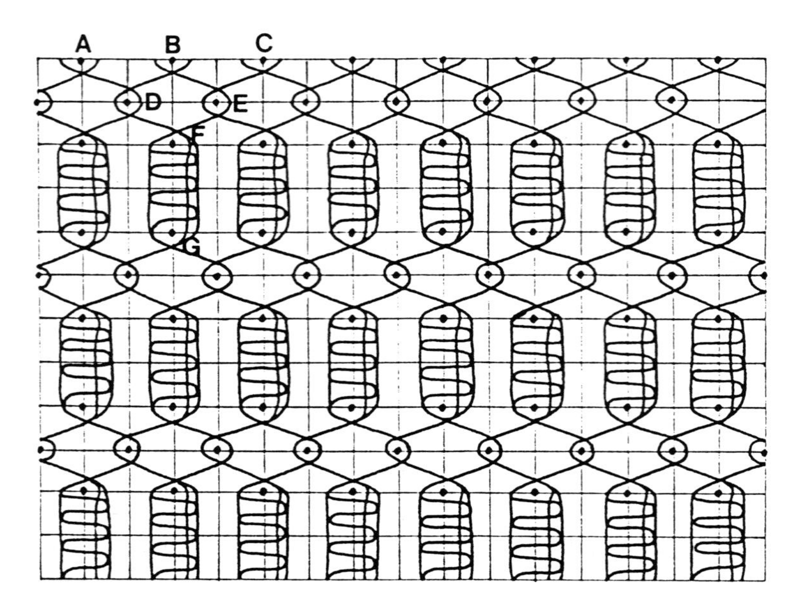

Taunton

This filling is a variation of Straight Pin or Cucumber.

1 Sew in two pairs above each hole.

2 Make a whole stitch, three twists, pin, whole stitch and three twists in each of the top holes.

3 With the right hand pair from (A) and the left hand pair from (B), make a whole stitch, three twists, pin (D), whole stitch and three twists.

4 Do the same with the right hand pair from (B) and the left hand pair from (C) to make pin (E).

5 With the right hand pair from (D) and the left hand pair from (E), make a whole stitch, three twists, pin (F), three twists (do not enclose the pin).

6 Using the two pairs from pin (F), make a leadwork reaching down to pin (G). Put in pin and twist both leadwork pairs three times, whole stitch and three twists.

9 Traffic Lights

(Toad in the Hole Variation)

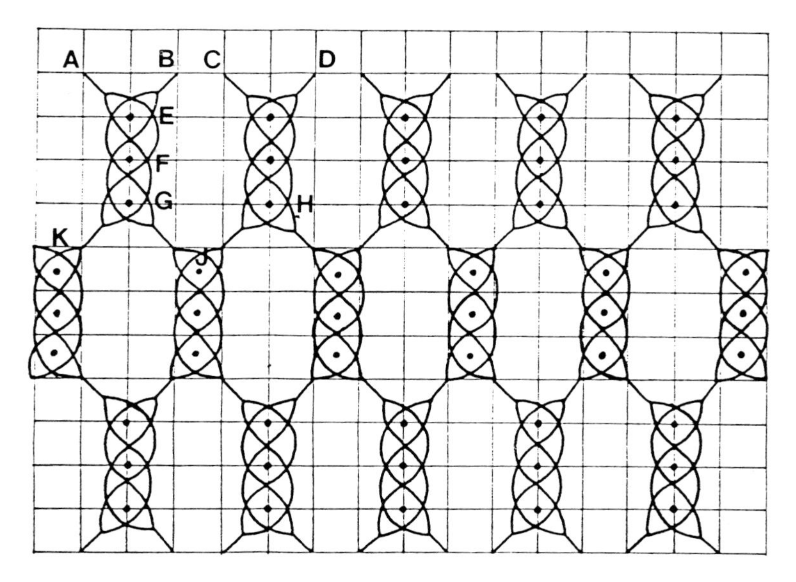

Traffic Lights

This is a variation of Toad in the Hole, but without the leadworks.

1 Sew in two pairs at (A) and (B). With the two pairs from (A) make a half stitch plait to reach as far as (E). Do the same with the two pairs from (B). Using these four pairs to form the Traffic Light, make a whole stitch and one twist with the middle pairs, and put pin (E) between them. Work a whole stitch and one twist with each of the two side pairs.

2 Work a whole stitch and one twist with the two middle pairs; put pin (F) between them. Work a whole stitch and one twist with each of the two side pairs.

3 Work a whole stitch and one twist with the two middle pairs and put pin (G) between them. Work a whole stitch and one twist with each of the two side pairs.

4 Enclose pin (G) by making a whole stitch and one twist with the two centre pairs.

5 With each of the two side pairs, work a bar of half stitches, to reach down to (K) and (J).

With the two pairs sewn in at (C) and at (D), work the three holes down to (H). The two left hand pairs from (H) and the two right hand pairs from (G) make up pinhole (J).

Devon County Show 1990, Third, Dilys Hendy

Bibliography

DEVONIA, *The Honiton Lace Book* (Paul P.B. Minet 1972)

EARNSHAW, PAT, *A Dictionary of Lace* (Shire Publications Ltd 1982)

HUNGERFORD-POLLEN, MRS JOHN, *Seven Centuries of Lace* (William Heinemann 1908)

LUXTON, ELSIE, *The Technique of Honiton Lace* (B.T. Batsford Ltd 1979)

LUXTON, ELSIE and FUKUYAMA, YUSAI, *Royal Honiton Lace* (B.T. Batsford Ltd 1988)
Flowers in Honiton Lace (B.T Batsford Ltd 1992)

MAIDMENT, MARGARET, *A Manual of Hand Made Bobbin Lace Work* (B.T. Batsford Ltd 1983)

PERRYMAN, PAT and VOYSEY, CYNTHIA, *New Designs in Honiton Lace* (B.T. Batsford Ltd 1984)

SIMEON, MARGARET, *The History of Lace* (Steiner and Bell 1979)

STOTT, GERALDINE and COOK, BRIDGET, *The Book of Bobbin Lace Stitches* (B.T. Batsford Ltd 1980)

TAKANO, SAIKOH, *Birds and Animals in Honiton Lace* (B.T. Batsford Ltd 1992)

THOMPSON, SUSANNE, *Introduction to Honiton Lace* (B.T. Batsford Ltd 1985)

Book Suppliers

Lynn Turner
Church Meadow Crafts
7 Woodford Road
Winsford

Creative Crafts &
Needlework
18 High Street
Totnes TQ9 5NP

Lacemaid
6, 10 & 15 Stoneybeck
Bishop Middleham
DL17 9BL

Doreen Gill
14 Barnfield Road
Petersfield GU31 4DR

Larkfield Crafts
4 Island Cottages
Mapledurwell
Basingstoke RG23 2LU

Needlestyle
24-26 West Street
Alresford

Ruskins
27 Bell Street
Romsey

Redburn Crafts
Squires Garden Centre
Halliford Road
Upper Halliford
Shepperton TW17 8RU

Craft Basics
9 Gillygate
York

Shireburn Lace
Finkle Court
Finkle Hill
Sherburn in Elmet
LS25 6EB

J. & J. Ford (*mail order & lace days only*)
October Hill
Upper Way
Upper Longdon

Needlewoman
21 Needles Alley
off New Street
Birmingham B2 5AG

Bryncraft Bobbins (*mail order*)
B.J. Phillips
Pantglas
Cellan
Lampeter
Dyfed SA48 8JD

Hilkar Lace Suppliers
33 Mysydd Road
Landore
Swansea

Mr Stephen Mobsby
Well Head Books
The Old Vicarage
Bourton
Gillingham
Dorset

Equipment Suppliers

United Kingdom

Central Scotland Lace Supplies
3 Strude Howe
Alva
Clakmannashire
FK12 5JU

J. & J. Ford (*mail order & lace days only*)
October Hill
Upper Way
Upper Longdon

Honiton Lace Shop
44 High Street
Honiton Devon
EX14 8PJ

Hornsby
25 Manwood Avenue
Canterbury
Kent CT2 7AH

T. Parker (*mail order*)
124 Corhampton Road
Boscombe East
Bournemouth
Dorset BH6 5NZ

Sebalace
Waterloo Mills
Howden Road
Silsden
W Yorks BD2 0NA

Doreen Gill
14 Barnfield Road
Petersfield Road
Petersfield
Hants GU31 4DQ

Stitches & Lace
Alby Craft Centre
Cromer Road
Eppingham
Norwich
Norfolk NR11 7QE

John & Jennifer Ford
'October Hill'
Upper Way
Upper Longdon
Rugeley

Elizabeth Knight
Lacemaking Supplies
18 Bridge Street
Olney
Bucks MK4 4AB

Felicity Warnes
82 Merryhills Drive
Enfield
Middlesex
EN2 7PD

Itsa Bobbins
G & R Downs
2 Ryll Close
Exmouth
Devon

Chiltern Lace Supplies
9 Taylors Turn
Downley
High Wycombe
Bucks

Mainly Lace
Moulsham Mill
Parkway
Chelmsford
CM2 7PX

Makit Direct Ltd
The Old Post Office
101 High Street
Offord D'Arcy
Huntingdon

Tim Parker
124 Corhampton Road
Bournemouth
Dorset
BH6 5NZ

Josy & Geef Harrison
The Whitehouse
Brickyard Lane
Theddlethorpe
Lincs. LN12 1NR

USA

Ms Holly Van Sciver
Van Sciver Bobbin Lace
130 Cascadilla Park
Ithaca, New York 14850

Belgium

Fresia Bvba
Groothandel
Kantklosmaterialen
Philipstockstraat 4
B 8000 – Brugge

Holland

Barbara Fay
Verlag &
Versandbuchhandlung
Am Goosberg 2
Gammelby

Theo Brejaart
P.O. Box 5199
3008 AD Rotterdam

Sources of Information

UNITED KINGDOM

The Lace Guild
The Hollies
53 Audnam
Stourbridge
W. Midlands DY8 4AE

The Lacemakers' Circle
49 Wardwick
Derby DE1 1HY

The Lace Society
Linwood
Stratford Road
Oversley
Alcester
War BY9 6PG

The British College of Lace
21 Hillmorton Road
Rugby
Warwickshire CV22 5DF

Ring of Tatters
Miss B. Netherwood
269 Oregon Way
Chaddesden
Derby DE2 6UR

United Kingdom Director of International Old Lacers
S. Hurst
4 Dollis Road
London N3 1RG

USA

International Old Lacers
Gunvor Jorgensen (Pres.)
366 Bradley Avenue
Northvale
NR 076647

Lace & Crafts magazine
3201 East Lakeshore Drive
Tallahassee
FL 32312-2034

OIDFA
(International Bobbin and Needle Lace Organization)
Kathy Kauffmann
1301 Greenwood
Wilmette
IL 60091

AUSTRALIA

Australian Lace magazine
P.O. Box 1291
Toowong
Queensland 4066

Index